The
World's Best
Joke
Book

The World's Best Jokes

Golf
Dirty
Football
After-Dinner

HarperCollins*Publishers*
77-85 Fulham Palace Road,
Hammersmith, London W6 8JB

www.**fire**and**water**.com

This paperback edition produced for WH Smith
by HarperCollins*Publishers* in 2001
3 5 7 9 8 6 4 2

The World's Best Golf Jokes by Robert McCune, illustrated by Peter Townsend
First published by Angus & Robertson 1988

The World's Best Dirty Jokes by Mr 'J', illustrated by Arthur Robins
First published by Angus & Robertson 1984

The World's Best Football Jokes by Edward Phillips, illustrated by Graham Morris
First published by Fontana 1991

The World's Best After-Dinner Jokes by Edward Phillips, illustrated by Graham Morris
First published by HarperCollins*Publishers* 1993

ISBN 0 00 761441 1

Set in Goudy

Printed and bound in Great Britain by
Omnia Books Limited, Glasgow

Contents

The World's Best Golf Jokes

"Hey, George, did you hear the awful news about John?"

The two golfers were talking over a drink in the club bar.

"No what happened to him?"

"Well he had a great round on Wednesday — under seventy I heard — anyway he finished early and drove home, and found his wife in bed with another man! No questions asked... he just shot 'em both! Isn't it terrible?"

"Could have been worse," George commented.

"How?"

"If he'd finished early on Tuesday, he would have shot me!"

"What's your golf score?" the country club interviewer asked the prospective new member.

"Well, not so good," replied the golfer. "It's 69."

"Hey, that's not bad. In fact, it's very good."

"Glad you think so. I'm hoping to do even better on the next hole," the golfer confided.

With all its rites and refinements, many believe that golf has a venerable history. But this is far from true. It was an accident that led to the beginnings of the game.

Out on the gentle heather-clad hills one memorable day a Scottish shepherd took a wild swing at a sheep with his crook. He missed. His crook cut under the fortunate beast and accidentally hit a small, round pebble which was so neatly clipped it flew in a graceful arc down the slope. The shepherd followed after and gleefully lined up the pebble for a second swipe.

"Wha hey," he cried in delight, "now let's see if I can't hit some rabbits in yonder wee holey."

A colleague on an adjacent hill noticed a flurry of rabbit fur and leaving his flock, strolled over for a closer view — conveniently taking his heavy crook with him.

Of course that was the end of shepherding on that day. The game of golf was launched at 10.15 a.m., the first lie about a score was told at 11.30 a.m. and at midday, the first golf joke was heard over lunch in the pub.

"Just got a brand new set of clubs for my husband."
"Oh what a good trade!"

Roger and Charlie emerged from the clubhouse to tee off at the first, but Roger looked distracted.

"Anything the matter, mate?" Charlie asked.

"Oh, it's just that I can't stand the club pro," Roger replied. "He's just been trying to correct my stance."

"He's only trying to help your game," Charlie soothed.

"Yeah, but I was using the urinal at the time."

Man blames fate for other accidents but feels personally responsible when he makes a hole in one.

"I claim damages," shouted the angry man hopping on one foot and holding his ankle.

The player whose ball had connected with the pedestrian was apologetic.

"But didn't you hear me call 'fore'?" he asked.

"Four! Four!" stormed the victim. "I won't settle for anything less than a fiver."

The sky above was blue and cloudless. Only a light breeze ruffled the treetops outside the window. If the judge had been a lawmaker instead of a law interpreter he knew he would be making laws forbidding court sessions on such glorious days.

"Well," he mused, dragging his eyes back to the court, "I guess there's no way out. I might just as well tune back in on the case."

"And in addition to that, Your Honour," the barrister for the defence was droning, "my client claims she was beaten into insensibility by a golf club in the hand of her husband."

"How many strokes?" murmured the judge absently.

"Mildred, shut up," cried the golfer at his nagging wife. "Shut up or you'll drive me out of my mind."

"That," snapped Mildred, "that wouldn't be a drive. That would be a putt."

When the Maharajah of Merchandani was taken suddenly ill during a holiday in England he was attended by a young locum filling in for the Wimpole Street surgeon. The Maharajah's appendix was deftly removed and the patient was beaming.

"You saved my life," he said to the young man. "Whatever you want shall be yours."

"It was quite simple really," protested the young surgeon.

"But I am a rich man, I insist," said the princely patient.

"Well, I'd love a new set of matched golf clubs," the young doctor admitted.

"Consider it done," came the stately reply.

The surgeon forgot all about this grand promise until some weeks later when he received this cable:

HAVE YOUR CLUBS BUT SADLY ALL NOT MATCHED STOP FOUR DO NOT HAVE SWIMMING POOLS STOP

Paddy was playing golf at a very exclusive club in County Kerry for the first time, and on the sixth hole he hit a hole in one. Jubilant, he walked down to the green and, just as he was taking his ball from the cup, up popped a leprechaun.

"Sor," the leprechaun bowed politely and continued. "This is a very exclusive course which has everything, including the services of a leprechaun if you make a hole in one in the sixth hole. I will be delighted to grant you any wish your heart desires."

"Saints preserve us," said Paddy in shock. But seeing the leprechaun waiting so patiently he thought for a minute then admitted shyly that he did have a wish. "I want to have a longer penis," he confided.

"Your wish is granted, Sor," the leprechaun said and disappeared in a puff of green smoke down the hole.

So Paddy headed back to join up with his friends and as he walked he could feel his penis slowly growing.

The golf game progressed and Paddy's penis kept getting longer and longer until it came out beneath his shorts and reached down below his knees.

"Hmmmm," Paddy thought, "maybe this wasn't such a great idea after all." So he left his friends and went back to the sixth hole with a bucket of balls and began to shoot. Finally he hit a hole in one, and by the time he got down to the green, he had to hold his penis to keep it from dragging on the ground.

But he managed to take the ball from the cup and sure enough, out popped the leprechaun.

"Sor, this is a very exclusive course," said the leprechaun bowing once again, "and it has everything including the services of a leprechaun... oh it's you again. Well what will it be this time?"

"Could you make my legs longer?" pleaded Paddy.

Errol Flynn and W. C. Fields played many games of golf together resulting in many marvellous stories.

On one occasion the legendary swashbuckler and the legendary drunk were playing when Fields dislocated his knee. Flynn helped him back to the clubhouse where the professional offered to push the knee back in.

"But it will be quite painful," he warned.

"Proceed, my good man," said W. C., taking a long swig from his indispensable hip flask. "Pain means nothing to me."

The pro took a firm grip on the knee and pushed hard. Fields let out a howl of pain.

"Easy, Mr Fields," said the pro. "My wife had a baby a couple of days ago and she didn't make half that fuss."

"Yes, but they weren't trying to push it back in," retorted Fields.

"It was golf that drove me to drink," the great comedian once admitted, "and you know, I don't know how to thank it."

On another occasion Fields was asked if he believed in clubs for women.

"Yes," he answered, "if every other form of persuasion fails."

The Monte Carlo golf course is famed for its glorious position high in the hills behind the town — a place of lush beauty and tranquillity unless your game is off. Charlie's game was!

Not one of his shots went right. At the eighteenth hole he made a last swipe at the ball, missed completely, and tore up about a metre of turf.

He then strolled disgustedly from the tee and looked down to the blue Mediterranean. Sailing boats were to be seen gliding about hundreds of metres below.

"How," demanded Charlie, "how can anyone be expected to shoot a decent game with those infernal ships rushing back and forth."

"Why don't you play golf with Captain Fortescue any more, John?" the young wife enquired.

"Well, would you play golf with a man who talks when you're putting, fiddles his score and moves his ball out of the rough when you're not looking?"

"Certainly not!"

"Neither will the Captain."

A group of golfers were putting on the green when suddenly a ball dropped in their midst. One of the party winked at the others and shoved the ball into the hole with his foot.

Seconds later a very fat player puffed on to the green quite out of breath and red of face. He looked round distractedly and then asked:

"Seen my ball?"

"Yeah, it went in the hole," the joker answered with straight-faced alacrity.

The fat one looked at him unbelievingly. Then he walked to the hole, looked in, reached down and picked up his ball. His astonishment was plain to see. Then he turned, ran down the fairway and as he neared his partner the group on the green heard him shout:

"Hey, Sam, I got an eleven."

An attack of grippe laid Snavely low just before his usual weekend game. He rested for a couple of weeks and looked forward to being back on the links. But just as he was about to play again, the grippe returned.

His regular opponent was miffed and grumbled at the other end of the telephone.

"Why can't you play this time, Snavely?" he wanted to know.

"Let me put it this way," said the sufferer sadly. "My trouble is an overlapping grippe."

What do you do when your opponent claims to have found his ball in the rough and you know he's a liar because his ball is in your pocket?

"I see a Russian says he has invented a game which closely resembles golf."

"Oh yes, my husband's been playing that for years."

A golf professional, hired by a big department store to give golf lessons, was approached by two women.

"Do you wish to learn to play golf, madam?" he asked one.

"Oh, no," she replied, "it's my friend who's interested in learning. I learned last Wednesday."

"I'd move heaven and earth to be able to break 100 on this course," sighed the veteran.

"Try heaven," advised the caddie. "You've already moved most of the earth."

"I gather you make more money in a year than Ronald Reagan," a nosey stranger asked a leading professional.

"Yeah, well why not?" came the reply. "I'm a better player than he is."

"If you spend so much time at golf you won't have anything laid aside for a rainy day."

"Oh won't I just! You should see my desk. It's just groaning with the work that I've put aside for a rainy day."

A visitor about to play the second dogleg at the Killarney Golf Club hit his ball into the woods. He went to retrieve it and came upon a witch stirring a large cauldron. As the steam billowed up, the man stood watching it transfixed.

"What's in there?" he asked finally.

"Ah, this is a magic brew," the witch cackled. "If you drink this, you will have the best golf game in the world! Nobody will be able to beat you!"

"I'd give anything in the world for that," said the man.

"Well you shall have it," replied the crone. "But I must warn you there's a penalty for having such power. You will not only have the best game in the world but you will have the worst sex life. Is that something you're prepared for?"

The golfer paused for a moment to consider; then, without a word, he held out his hand for a cup of the brew.

He returned to his game and immediately hit a hole in one. Soon after he became club champion, soon after that he became the best player in the country and soon after that he won every major international tournament there was.

A year later and now acknowledged as the world's best player, he was playing at the same course and he remembered his past experience. He decided to see if the witch was still there and indeed he found her still in the same place still bent over the cauldron.

"Ah, it's you," she said. "Tell me how is your game of golf?"

"The best there is," replied the man with honesty.

"Ah, and what about your sex life?" she cackled.

"Not bad," he replied.

"Eh? What's that? What do you call 'not bad'?"

"Well I had sex three, maybe four times last year."

"Three, four!" shrieked the witch, "and you call that 'not bad'!"

"As parish priest at Ballymooney, I find it not too much of a hardship."

The tall highlander walked into the shop at Pitlochry Golf Club and stood ramrod straight as he pulled a badly nicked ball from his sporran.

"What can you do?" he asked the manager.

"Well," said the manager in complete understanding, "we can vulcanise it for five pence or re-cover it for ten."

"I'll let ye know t'morra," said the customer.

The next day he was back, holding out the ball. "Tha' Regiment," he said, "votes ta' vulcanise."

"That's good for one long drive and a putt," said the cocky golfer as he teed his ball and looked down the fairway to the green. He swung mightily and hit his ball which landed about a metre from the tee.

His caddie handed him a club and remarked:

"And now for one hell of a putt."

"Can ye see your way to letting me have a golf ball, Jock?" Ian asked his old friend.

"But Ian, you said you were going to stop playing golf," said Jock reluctantly handing over an old spare.

"By degrees, Jock. By degrees," replied Ian pocketing the ball. "I've stopped buying balls as a first step."

Friendly golfer (to player searching for lost ball):
"What sort of a ball was it?"
Caddie (butting in):
"A brand new one — never been properly hit yet!"

He'd been marooned on the island for almost five years and had given up hope of being saved. He had resigned himself to living alone for the rest of his days without the solace of human company.

One day, however, a beautiful woman clad only in a wetsuit swam onto the shore of his island. She was the lone survivor of another wreck.

The castaway gasped and ran to meet her. Overjoyed at having someone to talk to he blurted out his whole story — how he'd managed to live off the land, surviving by his wits and so on. It was marvellous to speak with another human being.

"Good heavens," the woman cried breaking into his narrative, "you mean you've been on this island for five years?"

"That's right," said the man.

"Tell me," she asked in a husky voice as she brushed a blonde lock of hair out of her large and lovely eyes, "did you smoke cigarettes before you were marooned?"

"Yes, yes, I did," he remembered with pleasure.

"Well, since you haven't had a cigarette for so long, here!" and the beauty unzipped a pocket in the wetsuit and produced a packet of cigarettes which she gave to him.

As she leant close to light his cigarette for him the new arrival murmured, "Were you a drinking man before you got shipwrecked?"

"Well," said the man contentedly puffing, "I did enjoy the occasional whisky."

The woman unzipped another pocket and produced a hip flask which she offered him.

He took a pull from the flask and was thanking her when she leant closer to him and whispered, "You've been here for five years and in all that time I guess you haven't, um, played around either have you?" And as she spoke she began to pull down the zip at the front of her wetsuit.

"Good heavens," he said in high excitement. "Don't tell me you have a set of clubs in there as well."

Caddying for the elderly beginner had required great patience. He was doddery but he was dogged and he had sworn to break 100 before the summer was out. In fact there was a bottle of malt riding on it — his faithful caddie would receive it when the magic score had been broken.

Then arrived a day when dogged persistence seemed about to pay off for both player and caddie. They were on the green at the eighteenth and only 97 strokes had been accounted for. Player and caddie were excited and in the grip of such emotion it was small wonder that the player sent his first putt racing three metres past the hole.

In a flash the caddie had dropped the flagstick, picked up the ball and was crying excitedly.

"Well done, sir! You've done it! You've done it! Anyone would give you that."

Having led an interestingly dissolute life composed largely of women, drinking, gambling and golf, but not necessarily in that order, at the end of it, the new arrival was not too surprised to find himself in hell. He was however quite surprised to find that his particular corner of Hades was an eighteen-hole golf course complete with gentle woods, a cooly serene lake, well kept fairways, an immaculate green and a clubhouse with the usual professional's shop. The reprobate's delight was complete when he read the shop's notice.

HELP YOURSELF. ALL EQUIPMENT FREE.

"Well, this is going to be tough to take," he leered as he chose a bag containing perfectly matched clubs. So laden he ambled to the first tee where he took out a driver, gave a delighted practice swing and then felt in the ball pocket. It was empty.

He was about to return to the shop to remedy the situation when he noticed a grinning figure in red.

"Don't mind me," the grin grew wider, "and don't bother going back for balls. There aren't any. That's the hell of it!"

Morris was a man who knew all there was to know about golf. He knew all the courses, the champions, their scores, as well as the prize money the professionals had won for the past fifty years or more. He had read every book ever published on the game and knew all there was to know about technique, but, strange to say, he had never played a game.

Having listened to him hold forth for so long his friends finally ganged up on him and insisted that he play a game. It was arranged for the following weekend.

Morris set out with borrowed clubs and faced the eighteen holes of his home course. Five hours later he returned with a score of 63 which included four eagles, nine birdies and a hole in one. Never had anyone seen such a fine performance from a beginner.

However while the celebrations were going on in the clubhouse, Morris announced that he would never play again.

"What!" cried his distraught mates. "What!" echoed the equally distraught pro. "But you could win all sorts of prizes for the club. You know everything there is to know about the game."

"Not everything," Morris replied. "The books didn't tell me I'd have to walk."

Tickets for the British Open are hard to get and the touts have a field day. One keen spectator was offered a ticket for £50.

"That's absurd," the enthusiast declared. "Why, I could get a woman for that!"

"True sir, but with this ticket you get eighteen holes!"

Mulholland believed himself a superior caddie. He certainly had a superior attitude towards the man whose clubs he carried. Why only last month he had caddied for Lee Trevino, and now each time his client asked for a 5—wood, the boy would sneer, "Lee Trevino used a 4—iron from here."

And so it continued all the way around. The caddie recommended the clubs Trevino would have used and the golfer's game went rapidly from bad to worse.

Finally, at the eighteenth, there was a huge lake to cross.

"OK, know-all," said the golfer, "what would Trevino suggest here?"

"I think if Lee had come this far with you, he'd say, 'Use an old ball.'"

"When can you let me have another session?" a golfer asked his professional who was a veteran of 75 years.

"Tomorrow morning," came the reply, "but not tomorrow afternoon. That's when I visit my father."

"Goodness me," exclaimed the student incredulously, "how old is he then?"

"He's 95."

"And he's a good player too?"

"Ah no sir — he knocks the ball about a bit — but, bless him, he'll never make a player."

"My wife says that if I don't give up golf she'll leave me."

"Say, that's tough, old man."

"Yeah, I'm going to miss her."

"Now," said the golf pro, "suppose you just go through the motions without driving the ball."

"But that's precisely the difficulty I'm trying to overcome," said his pupil.

He'd sliced his drive and watched resignedly as the ball plummeted into the woods. He followed after and found his ball — surrounded by thick undergrowth and wedged firmly between two tree roots.

He contemplated the situation for a few profoundly silent minutes then turned to his caddie and asked:

"You know what shot I'm going to take here?"

"Yes, sir," replied the boy as he took a hip flask of malt from the bag.

"Caddiemaster, that boy isn't even eight years old."

"Better that way, sir. He probably can't count past ten."

It takes real commitment to play on the Royal Nairobi course. It is bounded on three sides by a wildlife reserve the wildlife of which do not necessarily feel hesitant about grazing on greens or golfers, according to palate preferences.

The young Mormon missionary had great faith — even as he sliced his tee shot into a pretty rugged area off the course. He knew he'd find his ball and he did — between the forelegs of a huge and hungry lion.

As he fell quivering to his knees before the great beast the young man began to pray and to his astonishment the lion knelt also.

"Glory be to God," exclaimed the young evangelist, "a practising Christian lion."

"Rowrrl," roared the lion, "quiet while I'm saying grace!"

Time for a quick moral observation, the parson thought as he watched his partner's ball fly into a devilishly tricky sand trap on the fourth.

"I have observed," he said, "that the best golfers are not addicted to bad language."

His partner swept a load of sand into space and, looking down at his ball still nestling between his feet, said:

"What in the bloody hell have they got to swear about?"

The new wife was trying to fathom the mysteries of the game that so occupied her spouse's time.

"What is a handicapped golfer?" she asked.

"One who plays with his boss," came the reply.

Rich Texans are fabled for their grand style but when one oil tycoon appeared at a local British golf course followed by a servant pulling a foam-cushioned chaise-longue, his opponents thought that this was taking style too far.

"J. R., are you going to make that poor caddie lug that couch all over the course after you?" he was asked.

"Caddie, my eye," explained J. R. "That's my psychiatrist."

Isn't it great to get out on the old golf course again and lie in the sun?

Women are cunning golfers: they shout "fore", hit 7, and score 3.

Two golfers, slicing their drives into the rough, went in search of the balls. They searched for a long time without success while a dear old lady watched them with a kind and sympathetic expression.

At last, after the search had proceeded for half an hour, she addressed them sweetly.

"I hope I'm not interrupting, gentlemen," she said, "but would it be cheating if I told you where they are?"

Nothing counts in a golf game like your opponent.

There was a bit of a queue beginning to form up at the Pearly Gates. "Something of a delay up front" was the word that went back to those waiting admission. St Peter was giving some new arrival a bit of the third degree.

"Yers," said that most venerable saint, "well despite what could be classified as an exemplary life, we do have record here of an occasion when you took the name of the Lord in vain. That'll need some explaining."

"Ah yes, I remember it well," said the mild-mannered applicant. "Pebble Beach Golf Course, 1962."

"Pebble Beach, eh?" said the saintly gatekeeper looking up with a start of interest from his records. "Difficult course, that."

"Yes indeed, sir. And that day I was on the last hole and only needed a par four to break 70 for the first time in my life."

"How was your drive?" St Peter asked sitting forward.

"Great, right down the centre of the fairway. But when I got to my ball it had fallen behind an empty Coke tin embedded in the turf."

"Oh dear," said St Peter. "Tight spot eh? Is that when you..."

"No, I'm OK with my irons. I managed to clip it neatly and it made the green but the wind caught it and rolled it off the lip and into a bunker."

"Ah," said St Peter. "Always was a windy course that. So that's when you..."

"No, no. It was still worth a try so I just dug in and

swung. The ball, plus a great quantity of sand landed on the green and the ball rolled to within 20 centimetres of the hole."

"JESUS CHRIST!" shrieked St Peter. "Don't tell me you missed the goddam putt!"

Meanwhile down below...
The Reverend Dolan was beginning to regret accepting the invitation to play golf with two members of his congregation. They had also asked the local golf pro to join them and, although the minister's handicap was respectable, his game was sadly lacking that afternoon. The pro was far from sympathetic and at every less than perfect stroke, sneered at what he called the minister's ungodly game.

He was still sneering back in the clubhouse and loud-mouthing the minister's mistakes for all to hear, when he delivered his final shot as the minister downed his ale and made to leave.

"Let's do it again, Reverend. If you can find anybody else to make it a foursome, I'd be glad to play you again."

"We might have a game next Saturday," replied the man of the cloth. "I doubt if any of my friends can play, but why don't you invite your parents and after the game I could marry them for you."

Greg Norman, in need of a well-earned rest, flew his family off to Nepal. But like any golfer on holiday, he had of course to try the local links — a mountainous course situated high in the Himalayas.

The club was delighted to welcome him but desolated that they couldn't provide a caddie as the Sherpas who usually attended were on an Everest expedition. However, they assured him they could provide a yak who would serve very well instead.

"Sahib Norman," assured the secretary, "this animal is of inestimable value but you have to watch out for him as he does like to sit on golf balls. It is, however, no problem as you have merely to reach under him and remove the ball. The yak will then continue on with the caddying."

Forewarned and only slightly perturbed, Greg set out. Over the first eight holes he had only had to remove the ball from beneath the sitting yak twice. Then on the ninth hole he had to drive the ball blind over a rocky outcrop. The yak took off after it and Greg followed the yak. He caught up with it beyond the rocks. It was sitting in a water hazard — right up to its neck.

Greg stripped off and dived in the icy water to rescue his ball. He groped around under the yak but could not feel it at all. He surfaced, took another deep breath and tried again. Still nothing. Almost frozen, he tried again but with the same result.

Finally he gave up and frozen to the bone made his way back to the clubhouse.

"Hey fella, what's going on?"

He explained to the secretary how he had dived three times for his ball but that the yak refused to move. He told the man how he couldn't find his ball and was

almost frozen to death in the process. "And," he went on, "that bloody yak is still sitting out there in the water hazard."

"Oh, a thousand pardons, Sahib." The secretary was very apologetic. "I forgot to tell you. That yak also likes to sit on fish."

"Hang it all, Harry, you can't expect me to pay that!" The two golfers were discussing a bill that Harry the hospital administrator had sent to Bill, a recent father for the first time.

"I mean Harry, £25 for the use of the delivery room. It's just not on, old man. You know I didn't get the wife there in time and the baby was born on the hospital's front lawn."

Harry leant over, took the bill, crossed out the offending entry and substituted another.

"Greens Fee £25," it read.

Which brings to mind MacDonald.

MacDonald was aged 80 when, for the first time in his life, he walked into his golf club bar and ordered drinks for everyone.

"What's the occasion, mon?" enquired the stunned bartender. "Hole in one?"

"No," the old highlander replied, "I've just married a bonnie lass!"

It was seven months later when MacDonald again strode into the bar and again ordered drinks all round.

"And what are we celebrating this time?" asked the amazed bartender.

" 'Tis the wife, lad, she's just presented me with a baby boy."

"But you've only been married seven months!"

" 'Tis true, 'tis true! Imagine it — two under par and me with a whippy shaft!"

"What's the matter?" Charlie asked impatiently.

Charlie and Jim were teeing off but Jim was rather a long time taking his stance.

"My wife came along with me today — she's watching me now from the clubhouse, and I want to make this next shot a good one," Jim explained.

"Good lord," Charlie exploded, "you haven't got a hope of hitting her at this distance."

He'd rejected the idea of dieting, health spas and swimming but when his doctor advised golf, the corpulent patient thought it might be worth trying. After a few weeks, however, he was back at the doctor's and asking whether he could take up some other game.

"But," protested the doctor, "what's wrong with golf? There's no finer game!"

"You are doubtless correct," the patient replied, "but my trouble is that when I put the wretched ball where I can see it I can't hit it and when I put it where I can hit it, I can't see it!"

"Honestly, I took twelve hours to play my round," a husband was explaining to his furious wife.

"What! For eighteen holes?" his wife asked in obvious disbelief.

"Well sixteen, actually. Browning died of a heart attack on the second and it's such slow going when you have to hit the ball, drag a body, hit the ball, drag a body, hit..."

"How many strokes d'ye have, laddie?" the Scot asked his guest after the first hole.

"Seven."

"I took six. Ma' hole."

They played the second hole and once again the Scot asked: "How many strokes?"

"Oh no sir!" said the guest. "It's my turn to ask."

Three visitors to the Royal Eastborne Club decided to join forces for a game but, of course, they first introduced themselves to each other.

"My name is Avram Solomon," said the bearded gent, "but I'm not the Rabbi."

"My name is Attila, but I'm not the Hun," said the quietly spoken youth wearing glasses.

"My n-n-n-name is M-M-M-Mary," said the shy young woman, "and I'm not a v-v-v-v-v-very good player."

It might have been Arnie Palmer or then again it could have been Gary Player — anyhow it was one of the famous professionals...

He hit his drive deep into the woods for the third time that day.

"The number four axe I think," he said with aplomb while turning to his caddie.

Saturday night and the clubhouse was crowded and noisy. The two players were drinking at the bar and discussing their game.

"Excuse me," the barman interrupted, "you're new members, aren't you?"

"Yes," replied one player, "but in all this crowd, how did you know?"

"You put your drinks down."

It was a heavenly day, enough to tempt the saints themselves from celestial chores and onto the links. And there was Jesus out on the course playing a few holes with St Michael as his caddie. As Jesus was about to make a drive He turned to St Michael and asked, "Which club do you think I should use for this shot?"

St Michael looked carefully over the course. "The 7-iron," he said.

"I don't know," said Jesus. "I think Jack Nicklaus would use the nine."

St Michael shook his head. "I think you'd better use the 7-iron, Jesus. Look, you have the sand trap in front of the green, and the lake beyond."

"Nah," said Jesus. "I think Jack Nicklaus would use the nine. Give me the nine."

So St Michael handed Jesus the 9-iron, and Jesus hit the ball. It went sailing out, bounced once on the green and then fell into the lake.

So they followed it down to the lake and, of course, Jesus walked across the water to find his ball.

A newcomer to heaven happened to pass by, saw Jesus walking on the water and asked St Michael, "Who does that guy think he is, Jesus Christ?"

"Naaah," said St Michael. "He thinks he's Jack Nicklaus."

Another day and the heavenly pair are at it again. While St Michael leant on his clubs, Jesus teed off. It was an awful shot. It screamed off the tee and disappeared deep in the rough. Then, suddenly a rabbit darted out onto the fairway with the ball in its mouth. Seconds later an eagle swooped down and carried the rabbit over the green. The rabbit squealed in terror and dropped the ball right into the cup. Hole in one.

St Michael turned to Jesus and said: "Look mate, there's money on this game. Now you gonna play or fool around?"

The secretary could see there might be trouble. The club's most straight-laced member was drawn against the bloke from Wagga whose language was so rich it would curl the tail feathers of a dead galah. The secretary took the Wagga wordsmith aside and pointed out to him how his language might give offence and begged him to try to modify it during the game.

All went well for several holes until, at the fifth dog-leg the bloke from Wagga hit his ball with a resounding whack right into the middle of the mulga.

It was too much for him and a string of colourful expletives reverberated over the course.

But quickly afterward he remembered himself and strode across the fairway to his opponent.

"I do beg your pardon," he said. "I bloody meant to say bugger."

Then there was the caddie with a similarly embarrassing vocabulary and reputation. He'd been assigned to caddie for the local Anglican bishop and warned by the caddiemaster to say nothing unless spoken to.

Things went well for a couple of holes. Then on the third the bishop's stroke was not quite clean.

"Where did that sod go, caddie?" asked the churchman looking to replace a divot he'd shifted.

"Into the bloody bunker," retorted the caddie who'd watched the ball, "and don't forget you started it."

"You think so much of your old golf game that you don't even remember when we were married."

"Of course I do, my dear. It was the day I sank that nine-metre putt."

Max had to admit it. There were many good things to be said about having a wife who was also a golfer. For one thing such wives understood and, for another, sometimes they could play a game together — as witness today.

They were teeing off from the eleventh when his drive veered from the course and came to rest behind the garage of a house built near the links.

It was his wife who pointed out that in fact the garage was directly between his ball and the links and that, rather than take a penalty he could try hitting it low with a 3−iron through the open garage doors and out the window on the opposite wall. Great idea.

Unfortunately his swing was a bit cramped and caught his beloved right between the eyes, felling her mortally in the instant.

About a year later he was playing the very same hole, this time accompanied by a caddie. Once again he sliced the ball and it fell almost in the same place.

The caddie pointed out that if he used a 3−iron and played a low shot through the open garage door and window opposite, there'd be no need to take the penalty shot.

"Oh no," replied Max, "not again. Last time I did that I wound up with a triple bogey!"

And speaking of games...

There was this Englishman and this Scotsman who were preparing to shoot a round of golf on the Royal and Ancient Golf Club of St Andrews. The Sassenach, a bow-legged squire from the Dales, stood near the tee while the Scot made a few practice swings. Then the bow legs proved too much for the Scot and obeying a mischievous urge, he sent the ball whistling between them.

"I say, old chap," the Englishman's tone was indignant, "that isn't cricket."

"No 'tis not," grinned the highlander, "it's good croquet, thought."

"I want you to know that this is not the game I usually play," snapped an irate golfer to his caddie.

"I should hope not, sir. But tell me," enquired the caddie, "what game *do* you usually play?"

47

On the seventeenth of the Wentworth Club Course a very careful player was studying the green. First he got down on his hands and knees to check out the turf between his ball and the hole. Then he flicked several pieces of grass out of the way and getting up he held up a wet finger to try out the direction of the wind. Then turning to his caddie he asked:

"Was the green mowed this morning?"

"Yes, sir."

"Right to left or left to right?"

"Right to left, sir."

The golfer putted... and missed the hole completely. He whirled on the caddie, "What TIME?"

"Well what do you think of my game?" the enthusiastic golfer asked his friend.

"It's OK, I guess," replied the friend, "but I still prefer golf."

The club secretary was apologetic. "I'm sorry, sir, but we have no time open on the course today."

"Now just a minute," the member rejoined. "What if I told you Mr Denis Thatcher and partner wanted a game. Could you find a starting time for them?"

"Yes, of course I would."

"Well, I happen to know that he's in Scotland at the moment, so we'll take his time."

After a three-month golfing tour in America the professional was at home in bed with his wife making up for his absence. Their romantic reunion was suddenly interrupted by a loud knocking at the door.

"Great heavens, that must be your husband!" cried the golfer, jumping out of bed and fumbling for his trousers.

"No, no. It can't be," replied the wife. "He's in America playing golf."

"You surely don't want me to hole that?" the pompous amateur blustered. His ball was about thirty centimetres from the hole but his opponent, a professional, answered quietly.

"No."

The amateur picked up his ball and walked on to the next tee. He was about to take the honour when he was interrupted by his opponent.

"My honour, I think," said the professional. "I won the last hole, as you didn't putt out."

"But you said you didn't want me to hole out," spluttered the amateur.

"That's right. I didn't. And you didn't."

"Good lord, Binky," the old admiral roared to his friend as he came into the clubhouse looking anything but pleased. "I've just been playing with a chappie from the Treasury. One of those civil service wallahs."

"Good oh, Bunny," replied the other old regular absently. "Bring him in for a drink."

"Can't," replied the old sea dog. "Playing the sixteenth someone shouted 'fore' and the blighter sat down to wait for a cup of tea. I've come in and left him sitting there."

Happily innocent of all golfing lore, Sam watched with interest the efforts of the man in the bunker to play his ball.

At last it rose amid a cloud of sand, hovered in the air and then dropped on the green and rolled into the hole.

"Oh my stars," Sam chuckled, "he'll have a tough time getting out of that one."

Same infuriating bunker, different infuriating spectator.

To Bill's wife, golf was a total mystery. She never could understand why Bill insisted on tiring himself by walking so far every time he played.

One day she went with him to see for herself what the game was about. For six holes she tramped after him. It was on the seventh that he landed in the infamous bunker where he floundered about for some time in the sand.

She sat herself down composedly and, as the sand began to fly she happily ventured:

"There, I knew you could just as well play in one place if you made up your mind to!"

He was a smooth operator, and at the club's annual dance he attached himself to the prettiest girl in the room and was boasting to her.

"You know, Jill, they're all afraid to play me. What do you think my handicap is?"

"I'd say your bad breath," came the quick response.

A little liquid refreshment at the nineteenth is of course all part of the game but the two Scots enthusiasts had partaken of nothing else but the national beverage throughout a long lunch break.

They returned to the links and played five holes before collecting themselves and their thoughts together.

"How do we stand, mon?" Jock asked.

"I dinna ken, Jock," Sandy spoke very carefully. "I'd say it was just a miracle."

It was a masterly addressing of the ball, a magnificent swing — but, somehow, a muddled slice shot resulted. The major's ball hit a man at full force and down he went.

The major and his partner ran up to the stricken victim who lay sprawled on the fairway. He was quite unconscious and between his legs lay the offending missile.

"Good heavens," cried the major with considerable alarm. "What shall I do?"

"We ought not to move him," said his partner, "so he becomes an immovable obstruction, and you can either play the ball as it lies or drop it two club-lengths away."

"If I died, would you remarry?" asked the wife.

"Probably would," came the reply.

"And would you let her be your golfing partner?"

"Yes, I think so."

"But surely you wouldn't give her my clubs?"

"Oh no. She's left-handed."

He was rolling in it. Made his money in scrap metal after the war and on retirement he had almost everything he wanted including time to enjoy himself — even time to take up golf.

He bought the best of everything he needed. Great clubs, shoes, sweaters as worn by the professionals, the lot, and he attacked his first game with gusto.

Behind him he left fairways looking like they'd been ploughed and greens looking like moles had surfaced in their hundreds. There were broken flag pins, clubs and mangled balls left in his wake, along with beercans, fag butts and a littering of discarded score cards.

His score was 285 which he celebrated over a steak and a pint.

"Excuse me, sir," a discreet voice interrupted his mastications. "I'm the convenor of the Greens Committee."

The novice looked around, his face filled with indignation.

"You're just the bloke I want to see. These brussels sprouts are cold!"

Then there was the New Zealander holidaying in Ireland and trying out Limerick's public course, famed for its difficulty.

Driving from thick woods on the twelfth, he aimed for the fairway but as he could not see it yelled "Fore!" and swiped. His ball struck a local player.

"Arrah, ye great mullock," cried the Irishman, as the Kiwi emerged in pursuit of his ball.

"But I called, 'Fore' and that's the signal to get out of the way."

"Well, when oi call, 'Foive,' that's the signal to punch your jaw! Foive!"

Overheard in the clubhouse bar:
    "Giving up golf, Andy! Have you lost interest then?"
    "Na, na. Lost ma ball."

"Why so sad?"
    "Doctor says I can't play golf."
    "He's played with you, too?"

"Did you hear about old Wilkins collapsing at the thirteenth hole?"
    "Yes, Herbert gave him the kiss of life and was drunk for seven hours."

"That can't be my ball, caddie. It looks far too old."

"It's a long time since we started, sir."

Father Patrick, who was not averse to berating his congregation for abusing the Sabbath, still liked to sneak off occasionally for a quick round of the course before the early morning service. At crack of dawn one midsummer morning he was spotted on the tenth tee one Sunday by an angel; and the angel was much annoyed.

"Father, he should be punished!" he said as he reported the miscreant to God.

"And so he shall be, my son. Watch this!" the heavenly Father replied.

Father Patrick hit off on the 590-metre, par five hole, and his ball arced gracefully in direct line with the pin. It dropped onto the green and a gentle breeze caught it and carried it a few centimetres right into the hole.

The angel turned a puzzled face to God. "Sir, I thought you were going to punish him and instead you've given him what every golfer dreams of — a hole in one and on the longest hole on the course!"

The good Lord smiled. "I *have* punished him! Who can he tell?"

"**I**'m going to have to give up golf," Mick sadly advised the club secretary. "I've become so near-sighted I keep losing balls and if I play with glasses they keep falling off."

"Listen, don't give up;" the secretary replied. "What about teaming up with old Bob Sullivan."

"But he's in his 80s and can only just make it around the course."

"Yes, yes, he's old, but he's also farsighted and he'll be able to see where you've hit your ball. It's a way to stay on playing."

The next day Mick and old Bob played their first game together. Mick teed off first and his powerful swing took the ball sailing up the fairway.

"Did you see it?" he asked Bob.

"Yes," the old-timer answered.

"Where did it go?"

"I forget!" came the reply.

A noted doctor's wife asked him why he never would let her play golf with him.

"My dear," he replied, "there are three things a man must do alone: testify, die and putt."

As he was walking his dog one weekday afternoon, J. P. Doneover, the bookie the punters loved to hate, espied a young lad upon the local links. J. P. stopped for a moment to watch him tee off and stayed for longer when he saw that the boy had talent. Indeed he had holed his tee shot.

He was about to call out his congratulations when the lad teed up again and once more holed in one.

Now J. P., never one to let an opportunity pass, walked up to the youngster, congratulated him and asked:

"How old are you, sonnie?"

"Eleven, sir," the young person replied.

"Anyone else here seen you play?" J. P. enquired.

Having received the assurance that no one had, J. P. proposed a match the very next day with the club champion lined up against the young tyro. The odds were handsome — 10 to 1 against the new young player.

The lad, however, took 11 at the first hole and went on around the course in much the same way. Of course he lost badly.

J. P. was furious. "You've made me look a right Charlie my lad. What's the idea of pretending you can't play?"

"Listen, dope," the youngster whispered, "next week you'll get 100 to 1."

"I'll go and ask if we can go through," said Max to Jerry.

The two golfers had been concerned for some time at the snail-like progress of two women, originally some holes ahead and now just in front of them on the ninth fairway.

Max returned after only a few paces towards the ladies.

"Jerry, this is very embarrassing, but would *you* mind going. That's my wife up ahead and she's playing with my mistress."

Jerry returned having got no further forward than Max.

"I say," he said, "what a coincidence."

"These are terrible links, caddie. Absolutely terrible."

"Sorry, sir, these ain't the links — we left them about forty minutes ago."

He'd been playing for twenty years and he'd never managed it — the ultimate goal, a hole in one.

As he was chipping away in a sandtrap one day and moving nothing but sand, he voiced the thought.

"I'd give anything," he said, "*anything* to get a hole in one."

"Anything?" came a voice from behind and he turned to see a grinning, red-clad figure with neatly polished horns and sharpened tail.

"What did you have in mind?" the golfer enquired.

"Well would you give up half your sex life?"

"Yes, yes I would."

"It's a deal then," and the figure faded discreetly from sight.

On the very next hole he did it. The ball just soared from his club in a perfect arc right into the hole. And for good measure, every other hole he played that round he holed in one.

As he was putting his clubs away the figure in red appeared once more.

"Now for our bargain," he said. "You remember you must give up half your sex life."

The golfer frowned. "That gives me a bit of a problem," he said.

"You're not backing out of this," cried the figure with a swish of its tail. "We'd struck a bargain and you agreed to it."

"Yes, of course. But I do have a problem. Which half of my sex life do you want — the thinking or the dreaming?"

Overheard on the links:
   "Your trouble is that you're not addressing the ball correctly."
   "Yeah, well I've been polite to the bloody thing for long enough."

That summer was a particularly hot one, but the Englishman who was on a golfing tour of the Continent gloried in the heat even though in Italy it had most of the locals gasping.

He was playing towards the fourth hole at Pisa's Golf and Country Club when he came across a player who was completely naked and cooling herself in the water hazard.

Being a discreet soul, he cleared his throat to let her know he was there. She took no notice.

"Er, I say, hello," he called hesitantly in case she hadn't heard his previous approach. "Er, I believe I've taken you unawares."

"Well," came a languid reply, "you justa' putta' 'em back!"

And talk about hazards...
    At New Zealand's Rotorua Club they include bubbling mud pools, quicksand and steaming geysers and the water hazards are hot and fast flowing.

A visiting American player on the twelfth came across a quicksand bog. Extending from it was a hand gesticulating wildly.

"My, oh my," said the Yank, "is he signalling for his wedge?"

A golfing clergyman had been beaten badly by a parishioner some thirty years his senior. He returned to the clubhouse, disappointed and a trifle depressed.

"Cheer up," said his opponent. "Remember, you win at the finish. You'll probably be burying me someday."

"Yes, but even then," said the cleric, "it will be your hole."

The schoolteacher was taking her first golf lesson. "Is the word spelled 'put' or 'putt'?" she asked the instructor.

" 'Putt' is correct," he replied. " 'Put' means to place a thing where you want it. 'Putt' means merely a vain attempt to do the same thing."

"You have got to be the worst caddie in the world!"

"Impossible, sir. That would be too much of a coincidence."

"You're late teeing off, Bill."

"Yeah, well it being Sunday I had to toss a coin to see whether I should go to church or come to golf."

"But why *so* late?"

"Well, I had to toss twelve times."

Frank joined a threesome; and as he'd had a very successful day he was invited back the next day for a game at 8 a.m.

"Look fellers, I'd sure like to play," said Frank, "but I could be two minutes late!"

Next morning he showed up right on time, played another lovely round but this time he played every stroke left-handed.

Again, he was invited to join the threesome at 8 a.m. the following day.

"Sure, I'll be here," said Frank, "but remember I could be late, but it will only be a couple of minutes!"

"We'll wait," one of the golfers assured him. "But by the way, could you explain something that's been mystifying us all. Yesterday you played right-handed and today you played left-handed. Obviously you're proficient at both so how do you decided which way to play?"

"Ah well," Frank answered, "when I wake up in the morning, if my wife's lying on her right side, I play right-handed and if she's lying on her left side, I play left-handed. Simple as that."

"But what if she's lying on her back?"

"That's when I'm two minutes late!"

By the time a man can afford to lose a golf ball, he can't hit that far.

The four friends were out enjoying a brisk game and were approaching the eighth hole, alongside which ran a main road. As the men moved on to the green a funeral procession moved slowly past along the road and one of the foursome removed his cap and stood with his head solemnly bowed as the hearse and accompanying cars passed by.

One of his friends noticed his action and was abashed.

"My gosh, Jim. You remind us all of our manners. It's not often though that one sees such a genuine gesture of respect for the dead."

"Oh, it's the least I could do," replied the man. "You know in six more days we would have been married twenty-five years."

"Caddie, why do you keep looking at your watch?"

"It ain't a watch, sir, it's a compass."

Judge: "Do you understand the nature of an oath?"
Boy: "Do I? I'm your caddie, remember!"

Then there's the one about the golfer and his caddie who enjoyed a good argument, especially about what clubs to use. The caddie usually won but this day, faced with a long short hole, the golfer decided that a 3—iron would be best.

"Take a spoon," growled the caddie.

But the golfer stuck to his choice and the caddie watched gloomily as the ball sailed over the fairway, landed neatly on the green and rolled politely into the hole.

"You see," grinned the triumphant golfer.

"You would have done still better with your spoon," came the dogged reply.

The lady golfer was a determined, if not very proficient player. At each swipe she made at the ball earth flew in all directions.

"Gracious me," she exclaimed red-faced to her caddie, "the worms will think there's an earthquake."

"I don't know," replied the caddie, "the worms round here are very clever. I'll bet most of them are hiding underneath the ball for safety."

Manchester to Melbourne, Perthshire to Palm Springs, the links on a Sunday morning get rather crowded no matter where and veterans throughout the world get irritated by delays.

Mackenzie and Brown were playing their usual weekend match on the links at Royal Sydney and were annoyed by an unusually slow twosome in front of them. One of them was seen to be mooching around on the fairway while the other was searching distractedly in the rough.

"Hey," shouted Brown, "why don't you help your friend find his bloody ball?"

"He's *got* his bloody ball," came the reply. "It's his bloody club he's looking for."

A golfer has one advantage over a fisherman. He doesn't have to produce anything to prove his story.

That he was a wealthy American tourist was obvious. On his arrival at a small Irish hotel the tiny reception area became full in an instant. Not only were there suitcases but also golf clubs, golf shoes, golf umbrellas and several boxes of balls.

"Surely now, sor," cried the manager eyeing the baggage with alarm, "there must be some mistake. We've no golf course you see and you'll be finding there's not one within miles of the place."

"Well now, that's no problem," drawled the tourist. "I'm having one sent over with my heavy baggage."

After a series of disastrous holes, the strictly amateur golfer in an effort to smother his rage laughed hollowly and said to his caddie:

"This golf is a funny game."

"It's not supposed to be," said the boy gravely.

At a Surrey golf club two sedate matrons were playing when a flasher rushed out of the bushes clad in nothing at all.

"Sir," asked the older of the two players severely, "are you a member?"

"My game's really improving, dear."

"How's that, Mavis?"

"I hit a ball in one today."

"Your ball hit me!"

"Not mine, it was my husband's."

"What are you going to do about it?"

"Want to hit him back?"

"Bill, I'm giving up, I've swung at that wee ball ten times and missed it every time."

"Keep trying dear. You've got it looking a bit worried."

"I say greenkeeper, I dropped my bottle of Scotch out of the bag somewhere on the seventh. Anything handed in at lost-and-found?"

"Only the golfer who played after you, sir."

The argumentative drunk in the club bar had been looking for a fight all afternoon since losing his game. Finally he threw a punch at the player on the nearest bar stool. He ducked and the drunk, losing balance, fell off his stool and onto the floor. By the time he'd disentangled himself from bar stools and dusted himself off, his opponent had left.

"D'ya see that, barman?" he complained. "Not much of a fighter was he?"

"Not much of a driver either, sir. He's just driven over your clubs," said the barman gazing out the window.

Explorer: "There we were surrounded. Fierce savages everywhere you looked. They uttered awful cries and beat their clubs on the ground..."

Weary listener: "Golfers, probably."

Paddy and Mick were returning to their native land to play in the All Eire Champions Golf Tournament. Halfway across the Atlantic the pilot of their plane announced over the intercom:

"Ladies and gentlemen. This is your captain speaking. I regret to say that we have lost the use of the outer starboard engine. But there is nothing to worry about. We still have three perfectly good engines which will get us to Shannon airport."

And an hour later the captain's voice was once again heard:

"Ladies and gentlemen. It's the outer port engine that's gone this time. But nothing to worry about, we still have two good engines."

Another half hour passed and once again the captain came on the intercom:

"Ladies and gentlemen. I do regret to announce that the inner starboard engine has gone . . ."

"Begorrah, Mick," Paddy turned to his mate with a worried expression. "If we lose that fourth engine, we'll not only miss the tee off, we'll be up here all night!"

"I've just killed my wife," cried the hysterical golfer rushing into the clubhouse. "I didn't see her. She was behind me you see," he sobbed, "and I started my back swing and clipped her right between the eyes. She must have died on the instant."

"What club were you using?" asked a concerned bystander.

"Oh, the No. 2 iron."

"Oh, oh," murmured the other, "that's the club that always gets me into trouble too."

Misjudging its depth, Ron went wading into the lake to retrieve his badly sliced ball. Very quickly he was floundering out of his depth and, as his tweed plus-fours became waterlogged, found himself in real trouble.

"Help, I'm drowning!" he shouted to his partner.

"Don't worry," came the reply. "You won't drown. You'll never keep your head down long enough."

The party games were a triumph and now the marble tournament was in full swing. Then six-year-old Simon missed an easy shot and let fly with a potent expletive.

"Simon," his mother remonstrated in embarrassment from the sidelines, "what do little boys who swear when they are playing marbles turn into?"

"Golfers," Simon replied.

Did you hear about the player who spent so much time in the bunker he got mail addressed to Hitler?

Golfer: "Notice any improvement today, Jimmy?"
Caddie: "Yes, ma'am. You've had your hair done."

Somehow it happened that Geoff, the Club's renowned drunk, ended up playing with Sister Mary Xavier from St Francis's Convent.

They were teeing off at the first tee. Sister Mary's drive was clean and straight. Geoff swung at the ball with an uncontrolled lunge. "Dammit," he said, "I missed!"

The good nun frowned but resisted the temptation to lecture.

Geoff took a second swing at the ball but again it was wild. "Dammit, I missed," he cursed.

Sister Mary looked cross but held her tongue.

Geoff's third swing chopped out a goodly quantity of turf but his ball remained immobile.

"Dammit. I missed again!" he shouted.

This was too much for Sister Mary. "Sir," she remonstrated, "if you continue to use such foul language the heavens may open up and the good Lord may smite you with a mighty lightning bolt."

Geoff stood swaying quietly listening to the good nun's message then once again he addressed his ball. Another mighty swing... and again he missed.

"Dammit. I missed!" he cried beating the earth with his club.

At that moment the heavens were rent with a fierce bolt of lightning which flashed down onto the course and hit... Sister Mary.

A mighty voice rang through the universe: "Dammit. I missed!"

A newcomer was to learn the great game at New Zealand's Otago Golf Club.

"And how does one play this game?" he asked his caddie.

The caddie explained about teeing off and the course and his clubs — the irons and woods and so on, but he finished by saying:

"Basically sir, all you have to do is hit the ball in the direction of that flag over there."

"Right ho," and the novice teed off. It was a magnificent drive that took his ball right down the centre of the fairway. And, unbelievably, it landed on the green only a few centimetres from the hole.

"What do I do now?" asked the novice.

"Just hit the ball into the hole sir," said the caddie in some excitement. "That's the whole idea of the game."

"*Now* you tell me!"

"I say, what happened to you, Carruthers?" enquired the secretary of the Berkhampstead Country Club.

The player whom he addressed was sitting staring morosely ahead, a neat whisky in one hand and his bandaged head in the other.

"Damned extraordinary business. Hooked me drive on the eleventh. Ball landed in the cow pasture beside the fairway. Couldn't find the damned thing."

"How very annoying. But what happened then? Did the cow have a go at you?"

"No, no. Was standin' there wonderin' when a memsahib playing behind me led off. Hooked her ball too... same direction as mine. So, thought... find her ball, find mine. D'y'see?"

"Do go on, old man."

"Lookin', y'see, and one of those damned cows walked past and swished up its tail... and there was a golf ball stuck firmly in place. Too far away though to know if my ball or the mem's."

"Yes?"

"Just then the mem jumped over the fence and asked 'Have you seen a golf ball?' 'Course I walked over to the cow, lifted its tail and enquired, 'Look like yours?' *That's* what happened to me!"

Eric, the club's worst golfer, was addressing his ball. Feet apart, just so, eye on the ball, just so, a few practice wiffles with the driver, just so, then swing. He missed. The procedure was repeated and then repeated again. On the fourth swing however he did manage to connect with his ball and drove it five metres down the fairway. Looking up in exasperation he saw a stranger who had stopped to watch him.

"Look here!" Eric shouted angrily. "Only golfers are allowed on this course!"

The stranger nodded, "I know it, mister," he replied. "But I won't say anything if you won't either!"

The old golfer paced anxiously up and down outside the emergency room of the East Lothian Hospital near Muirfield Golf Course. Inside the doctors were operating to remove a golf ball accidentally driven down a player's throat.

The sister-in-charge noticed the old golfer and went to reassure him.

"It won't be long now," she said. "You're a relative?"

"No, no, lassie. It's my ball."

Talk about fantastic golf teachers. He was the best and one day this woman came to him and said that she had developed a terrific slice.

Day and night he worked with her for five months. Now she's the biggest hooker in town.

At the Glenelg seaside course in South Australia a novice managed a mighty drive off the first tee. It hit, and bounced off in rapid succession, a rock outcrop, a fisherman, a tree trunk, the handle of a golf cart, a player on the second tee and finally it dropped onto the green about ten centimetres from the hole.

"Well," the player exclaimed, "if only I'd hit the bloody ball a bit harder!"

Bob and Ken had been friends for over twenty years and had played golf for over twenty years and, what is more, for over twenty years, Bob had lost each game. Well, that can only go on for so long — finally the worm has to turn and things have to change. Bob decided to get the greatest partner to help him beat the unbeatable Ken. So he found this giant Irish wharf labourer and got him on side.

They were out on the first tee with the hole some 400 metres off and the giant hit a tremendous drive which landed the ball on the green.

"I can't beat that," Ken moaned. "He'll probably go two on every hole. Here's the money. Incidentally, though, how does he putt?"

Bob carefully pocketed his win. "Same way he drives," he replied.

He was not what you'd call an expert player. Time after time he would hit his brand new balls where they couldn't be retrieved or even found. Balls went into the lake, out of bounds, across the highway, into the woods, and on one memorable occasion into a stormwater drain that was being built near the course.

It was after that shot that one of the members of his foursome suggested, "Why don't you use an old ball on those difficult shots?"

"An old ball?" the benighted player cried. "The way I play, surely it's obvious I've never had an old ball!"

His wife was a new and nervous player but Jim persuaded her to play against a new customer of his and his wife.

"After all," he explained, "it will be a two-ball foursome. I'll drive off and by the time you have to hit the ball the client and his spouse will be elsewhere on the fairway and not watching you."

It was agreed and the game started as Jim had said it would. He hit off with a fine drive, right down the fairway about 320 metres leaving about four metres to the green. He handed his wife an iron and told her to aim for the green. She sliced it with vigour into the deep rough at the side of the fairway. Two! His shot from the rough was magnificent and landed the ball back on the fairway — this time about half a metre from the green. Three! She whacked it right over the green and into the sandtrap on the other side. Four! He was in brilliant form and he clipped it neatly from the sand onto the green about a metre from the hole. Five! Her putt rolled off the green and into another sandtrap. Six! His recovery landed three centimetres from the hole. Seven! Her putt stopped at the green's edge. Eight! His putt of thirteen metres went in. Nine!

The customer and his wife holed out with four.

Jim's reaction was nothing too dramatic. He merely tore up his score card and ate it, broke three clubs and bent the remainder, jumped up and down on his golfcart and finally, shaking his fist at his wife, he strode off to the clubhouse.

His wife emerged from the sandtrap whence she had watched the performance. "I don't know what he's so mad about," she said. "After all, he had five; I only had four!"

An Australian touring round Britain was playing on a small course in Devonshire. He was on the first green and about to putt when he was suddenly beset by a flock of seagulls.

"Piss off, will ya'," he cried, thrashing at the birds.

A sweet little old lady who was sitting knitting near the green came over to speak to him.

"Excuse me," she said. "There's no need to speak to the little birdies like that. All you need to say is 'Shoo shoo little birdies!' Then they'll piss off."

"Let me inform you, young man," said the slow elderly golfer, "I was playing this game before you were born."

"That's all very well, but I'd be obliged if you'd try to finish it before I die."

Then there was the day the course was invaded by another al fresco diner.

An old tramp had wandered leisurely up to the green of the eighteenth where he sat himself down among his many coats. He dug among the variety of old bags he was carrying and brought forth with great pomp a handful of dried twigs and two iron rods which he arranged to form into a holder. From this he hung a pot of water suspended over the twigs.

Members gathering at the clubhouse windows watched as he got his campfire going. The tranquillity of the scene was shattered when a man dashed from the clubhouse and, leaving no room for doubt, ordered the tramp off the course.

"Well, just who do you think you are," asked the tramp.

"I'm the club secretary," shouted the man.

"Well, listen sonny," the tramp retorted. "Let me give you some advice. That's hardly the way to get new members."

As the two players approached the ninth tee they noticed what appeared to be a small picnic party assembled right on the spot.

"Here, what are you doing with our tee?" one called out.

"Garn, it ain't yours," came the retort. "We brought it wiv us all the way from Bermondsey."

Hempenshaw was playing off the sixth tee at the Royal Quebec Club. The fairway of the sixth needed some skill because it ran alongside the road. But Hempenshaw sliced the ball badly and it disappeared over the hedge bordering the road. So he put another ball down and took the penalty.

He was having a beer after the game when the pro joined him in the bar.

"Excuse me M. Hempenshaw, but was it you who sliced this ball into the road at the sixth this morning?"

"Yes, but I took the penalty."

"That's as may be, monsieur. But you might be interested to know that your ball hit and killed a small boy on a tricycle; the tricycle fell in the path of a mountie on a motorcycle. He skidded and was thrown through the window of a car, killing the nun at the wheel. The car then swerved into a cement mixer which wasn't too damaged but had to veer slightly and in doing so ran into the local school bus with such an impact that it sent it flying through the window of the St Lawrence shopping centre. At last count from the hospital there are thirteen people dead and seventy-nine people seriously injured."

The golfer turned a deathly shade of white and said, "What can I do?"

"Well, you *could* try moving your left hand a little bit further down the shaft," the pro advised.

Moishe and Abraham decided to join the best golf club that money could buy. On their first day they went into the bar for a drink before the game. They ordered two whiskies and enquired:

"How much is that?"

The barman smiled. "Are you new members?" he asked. "This your first day at the club?"

"Yes," replied Moishe and Abraham.

"Well, it's on the house."

Then the two friends decided to lunch in the club dining room. It was a sumptuous repast after which Abraham called the waitress over.

"We'd like to settle up," he said.

The waitress smiled sweetly and enquired whether they were new members.

"Yes," they told her, "we are indeed."

"And is this your first day at the club?"

"Yes," they replied.

"Then, it's on the house, sirs."

Much pleased, the two decided it was time to have a game so they walked into the pro shop to buy some balls.

"Give me half a dozen," Moishe ordered grandly. "How much is that?"

"Are you new members, sir? Is it your first day at the club?"

"Yes, yes," smiled Moishe.

"That will be seventy-five dollars," the pro advised.

Moishe turned to Abraham and whispered:

"It sure ain't by the throat they got you in this club."

Sam and Janet were beginning a game of golf. Janet stepped to the tee, and her first drive gave her a hole in one. Sam stepped up to the tee and said, "OK, now I'll take my practice swing, and then we'll start the game."

He had just come in from a long afternoon at golf. His wife kissed him and kissed their son who came in a few seconds later.

"Where's he been?" the husband asked.

"He's been caddying for you all afternoon," the wife replied.

"No wonder that kid looked so familiar!"

"Really, I can't play golf," said the blonde. "I don't even know how to hold the caddie."

Two long-time enthusiasts were discussing their scores over a beer in the clubhouse.

"I can't understand it one cried disgustedly. "I've been playing golf for fifteen years now and I get worse every year. Do you know, last year I played worse than the year before. And the year before that, same thing.

"That's depressing," commiserated the other. "How're you doing this year?"

"Put it this way," said the first, nursing his beer unhappily. "I am already playing next year's game."

Mark Twain accompanied a friend and watched while the friend played golf. Repeatedly during the game more turf was hit than golf balls and dirt went flying after every stroke.

Finally the friend turned to Twain and enquired how he liked the links.

"Best I ever tasted," came the swift reply.

Which possibly led Twain to the following conclusion:
Golf is a good walk spoiled.

The
World's Best
Dirty
Jokes

Reggie owned an elephant, but the cost of feeding it was getting out of hand. Then he got an idea. He had seen elephants lift one leg, and even two legs. Once in a circus he'd even seen an elephant lift three legs in the air and stand on just one.

So Reggie announced to the world that he'd pay ten thousand dollars to anyone who could make his elephant stand in the air on no legs. However, each person who wanted to try would have to pay a hundred dollars.

People came from near and far. They tried everything from coaxing to hypnotism, but no one could make the elephant rise up in the air.

Then one day a blue convertible drove up and a little man got out and addressed Reggie: "Is it true that you'll pay ten thousand dollars if I make your elephant get off all four legs?"

"Yes," Reggie said, "but you've got to pay one hundred dollars to try."

The little man handed Reggie a hundred-dollar bill. Then he went back to the car and took out a metal club. He walked up to the elephant and looked him in the eye. Then he walked behind the elephant and swung hard, hitting the elephant smack on the balls. The elephant let out a roar and flew up into the air.

After the little man had collected his ten thousand dollars, Reggie was very depressed. He'd only taken in eight thousand dollars and now he'd not only lost a couple of grand but still had the problem of feeding and housing the elephant.

Suddenly Reggie got another inspiration. He knew that elephants could move their heads up and down, but he had never seen one move from side to side. So he announced that he would pay ten thousand dollars to anyone who could make his elephant move his head from side to side. However, each person who wanted to try would have to pay one hundred dollars.

People came from near and far. They paid their hundred and they tried, but, of course, none succeeded.

Then just when things were going well, a familiar blue convertible drove up and the little man came out. He addressed Reggie: "Is it true that you'll pay me ten thousand dollars if I can make your elephant move his head from side to side?"

"Yes," said Reggie, "but you've got to pay a hundred dollars to try."

The little man handed Reggie the hundred dollars. Then he returned to his car and took out his metal club. He walked up to the elephant.

"Do you remember me?" he asked.

The elephant nodded by shaking his head up and down.

"Do you want me to do it **again**?"

The elephant quickly shook his head . . . no.

This man was in bed with a married woman when they heard the door open. "Oh my God," she gasped, "it's my husband! Quick, hide in the closet!"

The man hurried into the closet and closed the door. Suddenly, he heard a small voice saying, "It's very dark in here."

"Who is that?" he asked.

"That's my mother out there," the small voice said. "And now I'm going to scream."

"Please don't!" the man said.

"Okay, but it'll cost you money," the boy said.

"Here's five dollars."

"I'm going to scream!" said the small voice.

"Okay, here's ten dollars!"

"I'm going to scream," the small voice said.

"Here's twenty dollars."

Finally, when the boy turned down thirty-five dollars, the man said, "All I have is forty dollars."

"I'll take it!"

At last, the husband left and the man was able to get out of the closet and make a hasty exit.

That afternoon, the mother took the boy with her on a shopping trip.

"I want to get that bicycle," he said.

The mother said, "No, you can't. It costs too much money."

The boy said, "I've got forty dollars."

The mother said, "Where would you get forty dollars?"

The boy wouldn't talk. She began to berate him. He refused to respond. She slapped his face. He stood stoicly. Finally, twisting his arm, she dragged him into the nearby neighborhood church and approached the parish priest. "Father, my son has forty dollars and he won't tell me where he got it. Maybe you can find out?"

The priest nodded. He led the boy into a confessional booth. The boy sat on one side and the priest in the other. The boy said, "It's very dark in here. . . ."

And the priest said, "Now, don't you start that again!"

Then there is the story of the eighty-year-old Italian roué who called on his doctor.

"Professore, I would like you to examine me. To see if I am sexually fit."

"Very well, let me see your sex organs, please."

The aged patient replied, "Eccoli," and stuck out his index finger and his tongue.

A man who was frightened of dentists delayed seeing one until he only had six teeth left in his mouth.

The dentist examined him and said: "These teeth are finished. Let me pull them out. Let me do root canal work and all those other things I do, and you'll have a complete new set of choppers in your mouth. Beautiful you'll look, and chewing problems you'll no longer have."

The man was dubious. "I'm a physical coward, Doc. I can't stand pain."

"Who said anything about pain? I'm a painless dentist!"

"You say it, but how do I know if it's true?"

"Not to worry," the dentist said. "I did a job exactly like this for another man. I'll give you his name and you can phone him right now. Ask if I caused him any pain."

So the man telephoned George Kaplan in Brooklyn.

"Mr. Kaplan," he said, "my name is Al Goldstein. You don't know me, but I'm in the office of your dentist and he says he did a big job on your teeth. Is that correct?"

"Correct it is," Kaplan agreed.

"Okay," said Goldstein. "Now I want you to tell me the honest truth. Did it hurt? Tell me, yes or no?"

"A yes or no I can't give you," said Kaplan, "but I can give you a fr'instance. Every Sunday I go rowing in Prospect Park..."

"So?" said Goldstein.

"So," said Kaplan, "our dentist finished with me in December. Now it's June and it's Sunday, and, as usual, I'm in my rowboat on the Prospect Park lake. Suddenly, one of the oars slip away. When I reach over to grab it, my balls get caught in the oarlock. Would you believe it, Mr. Goldstein, it was the first time in six months that my teeth didn't hurt!"

An elephant was having an awful time in the jungle because a horsefly kept biting her near her tail and there was nothing she could do about it. She kept swinging her trunk, but he was far out of reach.

A little sparrow observed this and suddenly flew down and snipped the horsefly in half with his beak.

"Oh, thank you!" said the elephant. "That was such a relief."

"My pleasure, ma'am," said the sparrow.

"Listen, Mr. Sparrow, if there's anything I can ever do for you, don't hesitate to ask."

The sparrow hesitated. "Well, ma'am —" he said.

"What is it," said the elephant. "You needn't be shy with me."

"Well," said the sparrow, "the truth is that all my life I wondered how it would feel to fuck an elephant."

"Go right ahead," said the elephant. "Be my guest!"

The sparrow flew around behind the elephant and began to fuck away. Up above them, a monkey in the tree watched and began to get very excited. He started to masturbate. This shook a coconut loose and it fell from the tree, hitting the elephant smack on the head.

"Ouch!" said the elephant.

At which point, the sparrow looked over from behind and said, "Am I hurting you, dear?"

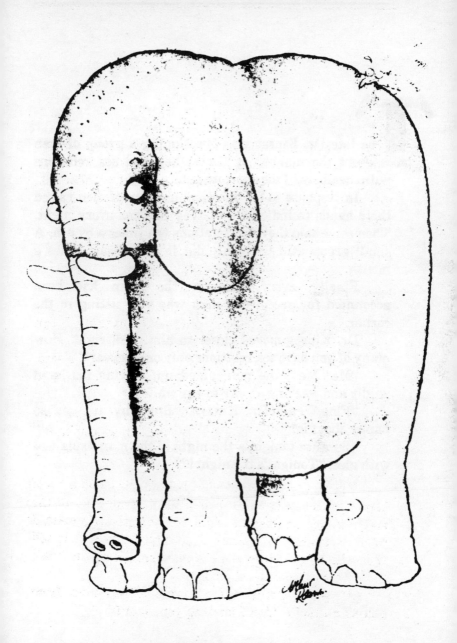

The late Dr. Kinsey was questioning a group of men about the number of times they had sex relations with members of the opposite sex.

In response to his question, a group of men raised their hands to indicate that they had sex every night. Then some said they had relations ten times a month. A small group said they only did it about four times a month.

Finally, every man in the room had been accounted for except one man who was sitting in the corner.

Dr. Kinsey moved closer to him. "All right. How many of you have sex relations only once a year?"

"Me! Me!" the man piped up, waving his hand wildly and wearing an ear-to-ear smile.

"Fine," said Dr. Kinsey. "But why are you so happy about it?"

"Because tonight's the night!" the man explained with glee. "Tonight's the night!"

So this old man went into Ma Agnew's whore-house and said, "Listen, Ma, I want a girl with gonorrhea."

The madam nodded and sent him upstairs to a room. Then she called one of her favorites for him. The girl came into the room and started to undress when he asked, "Do you have gonorrhea?"

"Gonorrhea? I should say not!" she said.

The old man sent her back. The madam summoned another girl and said, "Shirley, you go upstairs and tell this old codger that you have the clap. Okay? Let's do what we have to to make him happy."

The girl agreed and went upstairs, and when the old man asked, "Do you have gonorrhea?" she smiled and said, "Of course I do!"

"Good!" he said. "Let's get it on."

They got into bed together and fucked for about ten minutes. When it was over and they lay side by side, the girl named Shirley said, "Listen, grandpa, I've got a confession to make. I don't really have gonorrhea."

The old man smiled. "Now you do," he said.

He went to his doctor full of anger. "Doc," he said, "I feel like killing my wife. You've got to help me. You've got to tell me what to do."

The doctor decided on how to best handle the case. "Look," he said, "here are some pills. You take these twice a day and they'll enable you to fuck your wife six times a day. If you do this for thirty days, you'll fuck her to death."

"Wonderful, doc," said the grateful patient. "I think I'll take her to Miami Beach so there won't be anything to interfere with us and no one will be suspicious."

He left with a bottle of pills in his hand and a smile on his face.

Nearly a month passed. The doctor flew to Miami Beach for a medical convention. There, on Lincoln Road, he saw his patient coming along in a wheelchair, just managing to move forward.

"What happened?" the doctor asked. "What happened?"

"Don't worry, doc," the patient reassured him, "two more days and she'll be dead."

An old man made it shakily through the door to Joe Conforte's Mustang Ranch, outside Reno, Nevada.

The receptionist stared at him. "You gotta be in the wrong place," she exclaimed. "What are you looking for?"

"Ain't this the famous Mustang? Ain't this where you allus got forty-five girls ready 'n' able?"

The receptionist looked perplexed. "Ready for what?"

"I want a girl," the old man rasped. "I wanna get laid."

"How old are you, Pop?" she asked.

"Ninety-two," he replied.

"Ninety-two? Pop, you've *had* it!"

"Oh," said the old man, a little disconcerted as his trembling fingers reached for his wallet. "How much do I owe you?"

The scene was Elaine's Restaurant on Second Avenue in Manhattan on a crowded Saturday night. A stranger walked in from the street and pompously announced that, even with a blindfold on, he could identify any wine.

The challenge was immediately accepted. A dark cloth was placed over his eyes and wine after wine was handed to him.

"Lafite-Rothschild, 1958," he would announce. Or, "Bernkasteler Badstube, 1951." And he was always right.

Finally, someone handed him a glass he couldn't identify. He sipped, and then he sipped again. Suddenly he spat it out and pulled off the blindfold.

"Hell, man! This is urine! Plain fresh urine!"

"Yes," said a small voice in the background, "but whose?"

This gay chap was looking in a sex shop window. He saw a large rubber cock that appealed to him, and he ventured inside.

When the clerk came to wait on him, he pointed to the big black penis in the window. "I'll take that one," he said.

"Should I wrap it or just put it in a bag?" asked the clerk.

"Neither," said the customer. "I'll just eat it right here."

Jim and Joe were two friends who shared an apartment together in Chicago. One day, Jim came home to find Joe weeping into his hands. "I'm so unlucky! So unlucky!" he moaned.

"You're always saying that, and it isn't so," Jim said.

"It is! It is!" Joe said. "I'm the most unlucky fellow you know!"

"What happened now?"

"Well, I met this beautiful woman on Madison Street. We got to talking and we stopped off at a small bar and had a few drinks. Wow! We got really mellow. When she suggested that I go to her place, I thought my luck had changed."

"It sounds like it did," Jim said.

"Minutes after we entered her apartment I was in bed with her. I was just starting to climax when we heard the door bang open."

"It's my husband!" she said.

"I didn't even have time to grab a towel. I bounded for the window and just managed to climb out, hanging on the ledge by my hands, when he barged in.

"He sized up the scene immediately, and then he saw my hands hanging on for dear life. He came to the window and started pounding my knuckles with a hammer. Then he took out his cock and pissed all over me. Then he slammed the window on my bloody fingers.

Then, as if I didn't have trouble enough, two old ladies on the street saw me hanging there stark naked, and they started screaming for the police. The cops came and I was arrested. Now do you see what I mean when I say I'm unlucky?"

"Nonsense," Jim said. "You're upset, but an experience like that could happen to anyone."

"You don't understand," Joe said, "When the cops came to arrest me, I looked down and my feet were only four inches from the ground. Now do you see what I mean when I say I'm unlucky?"

Jones took his nymphomaniac wife to the doctor for treatment. "This is one hot potato of a lady, doctor," he said. "Maybe you can do something for her? She goes for any man, and I get very jealous."

"We'll see," the doctor said. He directed Mrs. Jones into his examining room, closed the door behind him and told her to undress. Then he told her to get up onto the examining table on her stomach.

The moment he touched her buttocks, she began to moan and squirm. It was too much for him to resist, and he climbed up on top of her and began to screw her.

Jones suddenly heard moans and groans coming from the examination room. Unable to control himself, he pushed open the door, to be confronted by the sight of the doctor astride his wife and banging away.

"Doctor, what are you doing?" he asked.

The flustered doctor said, "Oh, it's you, Jones? I'm only taking your wife's temperature!"

Jones opened his switchblade knife and began to hone it on his sleeve very deliberately. "Doc," he said, "when you take that thing out, it better have numbers on it!"

A midget went into a whorehouse. None of the girls really wanted to serve him, so finally they drew lots and Mitzi was unlucky and went up to the room with him.

A minute later, there was a loud scream. The Madam and all of the girls charged up the staircase and into the room. Mitzi lay on the floor in a dead faint. Standing next to the bed was the midget, nude, and with a three foot cock hanging down and almost touching the floor.

The girls were dumbfounded by the sight. Finally, one of them regained her composure to say, "Sir, would you mind if we felt it? We've never seen anything like that before."

The midget sighed. "Okay, honey. But only touching. No sucking. I used to be six feet tall."

A ventriloquist was driving in the country when he was attracted to a large farm. He asked for and was given a tour.

As he was shown through the barn, the ventriloquist thought he'd have some fun. He proceeded to make one of the horses talk.

The hired hand, wide-eyed with fear, rushed from the barn to the farmer. "Sam," he shouted, "those animals are talking! If that little sheep says anything about me, it's a damned lie!"

The salesman stopped at a farmhouse one evening to ask for room and board for the night. The farmer told him there was no vacant room.

"I could let you sleep with my daughter," the farmer said, "if you promise not to bother her."

The salesman agreed.

After a hearty supper, he was led to the room. He undressed in the dark, slipped into bed, and felt the farmer's daughter at his side.

The next morning he asked for his bill.

"It'll be just two dollars, since you had to share the bed," the farmer said.

"Your daughter was very cold," the salesman said.

"Yes, I know," said the farmer. "We're going to bury her today."

Charlie was visiting an old friend and his wife for dinner. When the time came to leave, his car wouldn't start, and it was too late to call the local service station.

The husband urged Charlie to stay over. There was no spare bed in the house; there wasn't even a sofa. So Charlie would have to sleep with the husband and wife.

No sooner had the husband fallen asleep when the wife tapped Charlie on the shoulder and motioned for him to come over to her.

"I couldn't do that," he whispered. "Your husband is my best friend!"

"Listen, sugar," she whispered back, "there ain't nothing in the whole wide world could wake him up now."

"I can't believe that," Charlie said. "Certainly if I get on top of you and screw you, he'll wake up, won't he?"

"Sugar, he certainly won't. If you don't believe me, pluck a hair out of his asshole and see if that wakes him."

Charlie did just that. He was amazed when the husband remained asleep. So he climbed over to the wife's side of the bed and fucked her. When he finished, he climbed back to his own side. It wasn't long before she tapped him on the shoulder and beckoned him over again. Again he pulled a hair to determine if his old friend was asleep. This went on eight times during the night. Each time Charlie screwed the woman, he first pulled out one of the husband's asshole hairs.

The ninth time he pulled a hair, the husband awoke and muttered: "Listen, Charlie, old pal, I don't mind you fucking my wife, but for Pete's sake, stop using my ass for a scoreboard!"

Muldoon had died from dysentery. When they went to prepare him for burial, he was still excreting. The undertaker thought about it for a moment, then went out and returned with a large cork. He corked up Muldoon's ass.

A couple of hours later, O'Shawnessy and Ryan came to carry the body down to the living room for the wake.

Ryan led the way as they started walking down the stairs slowly. Soft organ music was playing in the background and all the guests stood about with their heads bowed.

Suddenly, the cork came out and excretion came pouring down on top of Ryan's head. He promptly dropped the body and Culdoon's corpse came hurtling down the stairs.

The undertaker rushed up to Ryan. "What the hell did you do, man?"

And Ryan said calmly, "Listen, man, if that bastard can shit, he can walk!"

When the delegate from the emerging African nation was in Moscow, he watched a game of Russian roulette. Someone put the barrel of a pistol to his head and pulled the trigger. One of the six chambers contained a real bullet.

Now the Russian delegate was visiting the African nation.

"We would like to show you our version of roulette," the Ambassador said. "We call this African roulette."

"How do you play it?"

The Ambassador pointed to six buxom African girls sitting in a circle. "Any of these girls will give you a blow job."

"Where is the roulette part? Where is the jeopardy?" the Russian asked.

"Well," said the African Ambassador, "one of the girls is a cannibal."

Little Willie had a gambling problem. He'd bet on anything. One day, Willie's father consulted his teacher.

The teacher said, "Mr. Gaines, I think I know how to teach Willie a real lesson. We'll trap him into a big wager that he'll lose."

Willie's father agreed to cooperate with the plan.

The next day at school, the teacher watched Willie making wagers with the other children, and she said, "Willie, I want you to remain after class."

When the others had left the classroom, Willie walked up to the teacher. Before she could open her mouth, he said, "Don't say it, Miss B.; I know what you're going to say, but you're a liar!"

"Willie!" the startled teacher said. "What are you talking about?"

"You're a fake!" Willie continued. "How can I believe anything you tell me? You've got this blond hair on top, but I ve seen your bush and it's pitch black!"

Trying to keep her cool, the teacher said, "Willie, that isn't true."

"I'll bet a dollar it is!" Willie challenged.

The teacher saw her chance to teach Willie his lesson. "Make it five dollars and you have a bet," she said.

"You're on!" Willie whipped out a five-dollar bill.

Before anyone could come into the room, Miss B.

dropped her panties, spread her legs, and showed Willie that her pubic hair was as blond as the hair on top of her head.

Willie hung his head. "You win,' he said, handing her the fiver.

Miss B. couldn't wait for him to leave so she could get to a phone to call his father. She reported what had happened. "Mr. Gaines," she said, "I think we've finally taught him his lesson."

"The hell we have,' the father muttered. "This morning Willie bet me ten dollars that he'd see your cunt before the day was over."

The famous Greek ship owner, Ori Oristotle, was having a house built on a large piece of land in Greece. He said to the architect, "Don't disturb that tree over there because directly under that tree is where I had my first sex.

"How sentimental, Mr. Oristotle," the architect said. "Right under that tree."

"Yes," continued Ori Oristotle, "And don't touch that tree over there either. Because that's where her mother stood watching while I was having my first sex."

"Her mother just stood there while you were fucking her daughter?" the architect asked.

"Yes," said the Greek ship owner.

"But, Mr. Oristotle, what did her mother say?"

"Baaaa."

Mrs. Keller had a very talented parrot. At her dinner parties he was the center of attention, for she had trained him to repeat what the butler said when he announced the guests as they arrived.

The parrot had only one failing: He loved to fuck chickens. Every chance he got, he would fly over the fence into the yard of the farmer next door and fuck his chickens.

The farmer complained to Mrs. Keller, and finally she laid the law down to the parrot.

"Bertram," she said, "you better listen to me! The next time you go into Farmer Whalen's yard and fuck another chicken I'm going to punish you plenty!"

The parrot hung his head to show he understood. But two days later, he couldn't resist temptation and over the fence he went. He was deep into screwing his third hen when Farmer Whalen spotted him and chased him. Whalen complained again to Mrs. Keller.

"Now you're going to get it!" she said. She got a pair of barber's shears and clipped all the feathers from the top of the parrot's head.

That night, Mrs. Keller threw one of her gala parties. She put the parrot on top of the piano.

"Bertram," she said, "you've been a rotten old thing. Tonight you're to sit here all night. No wandering around and no playing the way you usually do!"

And so, feeling rather disconsolate, the parrot sat on the piano. As the butler announced the guests, Bertram performed as usual, repeating the names. The butler said, "Mr. Arnold Levy and Lady Stella," and the parrot said, "Mr. Arnold Levy and Lady Stella." The butler said, "Mr. and Mrs. Robert Salomon," and the parrot said, "Mr. and Mrs. Robert Salomon."

Then two bald-headed men entered the room. Without waiting for the butler to announce them, the parrot shouted: "All right, you chicken-fuckers! Up here on the piano with me!"

A farmer sent his fifteen-year-old son to town and, as a birthday present, handed him a duck. "See if you can get a girl in exchange for this," he said.

The lad met a prostitute and said, "It's my birthday and all I've got is this duck? Would you be willing to —?"

"Sure," she said. "I'm sentimental about birthdays. And besides, I've never owned a duck."

Afterwards, she said, "Do you know, for a fifteen-year-old, you're quite a lay. If you do it again, I'll give you back your duck. '

"Sure," said the boy.

When his pleasurable work was through, he started on his way home. While he was crossing the main street in the village, the duck suddenly flew out of his hands and was hit by a passing beer truck. The driver of the truck felt sorry for the boy and gave him $2.

When he got home, his father asked, "How did you make out?"

The son said: "I got a fuck a duck, a duck for a fuck, and two dollars for a fucked-up duck."

Lee and Larry were a pair of winos. They woke up with the shakes one afternoon to find they had only forty cents between them. Lee began to climb the walls, but Larry said calmly, "Look, old man, give me the forty cents and I'll show you how we can drink free all day." So they went into a delicatessen, and Lee bought a frankfurter, which he stuck in Larry's fly.

Next, they went into a nearby bar and ordered drinks. When the bartender asked for his money, Lee got down on the floor and started sucking the frankfurter. The bartender screamed, "You fucking queers, get out of here!"

They repeated the scene in bar after bar until they had toured a dozen of them. Finally, Lee complained, "Listen, Larry, it was a great scheme but my knees are getting sore from hitting the floor so much."

Larry shook his head. "You should complain," he said. "We lost the hot dog after the second bar!"

nflation was getting out of hand so Joe suggested to his wife, Louise, that they try a unique way to save some money on the side.

"Every time I lay you, I'll give you a dollar for your piggy bank," he said.

A few weeks later, they decided to open the piggy bank. Out tumbled a bunch of dollars, but these were mixed with a rich cluster of fives, tens and twenties.

"Louise," asked Joe, "where did you get all that money? Each time we fucked I only gave you a dollar.'

"So?" she said. "Do you think everyone is as stingy as you?"

The agent for a beautiful actress discovered one day that she had been selling her body at a hundred dollars a night.

The agent, who had long lusted for her, hadn't dreamed that she had been so easily obtainable. He approached her, told her how much she turned him on and how much he wanted to make it with her.

She agreed to spend the night with him, but said he would have to pay her the same hundred dollars that the other customers did.

He scratched his head, considered it, and then asked, "Don't I even get my agent's ten percent as a deduction?"

"No siree," she said. "If you want it, you're going to have to pay full price for it, just like the other Johns."

The agent didn't like that at all, but he agreed.

That night, she came to his apartment after her performance at a local night club. The agent screwed her at midnight, after turning out all the lights.

At 1 A.M., she was awakened again. Again she was vigorously screwed. In a little while, she was awakened again, and again she was screwed. The actress was impressed with her lover's vitality.

"My God," she whispered in the dark, "you are

virile. I never realized how lucky I was to have you for my agent."

"I'm not your agent, lady," a strange voice answered. "He's at the door taking tickets!"

A drunk walked into a bar crying. One of the other men at the bar asked him what happened.

"I did a horrible thing," sniffled the drunk. "Just a few hours ago I sold my wife to someone for a bottle of scotch."

"That *is* awful," said the other guy. "And now she's gone and you want her back, right?"

"Right," said the drunk, still crying.

"You're sorry you sold her because you realized too late that you love her, right?"

"Oh, no," said the drunk. "I want her back because I'm thirsty again!"

The butcher lived in an apartment over his shop. One night he was awakened by strange noises coming from below. He tiptoed downstairs and observed that his 19-year-old daughter was sitting on the chopping block and masturbating with a liverwurst. He sighed and tiptoed back to bed.

The next morning, one of his customers came in and asked for some liverwurst. The butcher explained that he didn't have any.

The lady was annoyed. She pointed and said, "No liverwurst, eh? Well, what's that hanging on the hook right over there?"

The butcher frowned at her and replied, "That, lady, is my son-in-law."

The couple visited a sex clinic to complain that their sex life had become a bore.

Each night the man would arrive home. His wife would prepare supper. After supper, they'd watch two hours of TV. Immediately after the eleven o'clock news, they would get into bed. From that point on, every move was routine.

"No wonder," the sex consultant said. "You've made sex monotonous. Stop living on a schedule. Get into sex when you feel like it. Don't wait until eleven o'clock each night. Do it when you get into the mood."

The couple agreed to try the advice. They returned the following week.

"How did things work out?" the sex doctor asked.

The man and his wife were beaming. "It worked! It worked!"

"Tell me about it," said the doctor.

"Well, two nights after we saw you, we were eating supper when I noticed that although it was only eight-thirty, I had this great erection. Sweetie pie here was staring at it with longing eyes. So I didn't wait for any shower or any news broadcast. Instead, I reached out, ripped off her blouse and her bra. Then I pulled off her panties. I flung her to the floor right under the table. Then I unzipped my fly and pulled out my cock and we began to fuck. Man, we fucked like we have **never fucked before.**"

"That's wonderful!" said the sex expert. "I told you it would work if you did it when the spirit moved!"

"Only one thing," the man said a little sadly. "They're not going to let us come back to Howard Johnson's restaurant any more."

Amother and her daughter came to the doctor's office. The mother asked the doctor to examine her daughter.

"She has been having some strange symptoms and I'm worried about her," the mother said.

The doctor examined the daughter carefully. Then he announced, "Madam, I believe your daughter is pregnant."

The mother gasped. "That's nonsense!" she said. "Why, my little girl has nothing whatsoever to do with men." She turned to the girl. "You don't, do you, dear?"

"No, Mumsy," said the girl. "Why, you know that I have never so much as kissed a man!"

The doctor looked from mother to daughter, and back again. Then, silently he stood up and walked to the window. He stared out. He continued staring until the mother felt compelled to ask, "Doctor, is there something wrong out there?"

"No, Madam," said the doctor. "It's just that the last time anything like this happened, a star appeared in the East and I was looking to see if another one was going to show up. '

The state senator was seeking votes for his election campaign for Congress and decided to visit the local Indian reservation. He stood in the large community hall and told the Indians what he would do for them if he was elected.

"I think the time has come when you people deserve to really control your own destiny," he said.

From the crowded auditorium came a responding chorus, "Um gwalla gwalla!"

The senator smiled. "Furthermore," he continued, "I think the time has come for your old people to get really good pensions."

Again came a chorus of "Um gwalla gwalla!"

He nodded approvingly. "One more thing," he said, "if I m elected, I'm not going to rest until every one of you Indians gets full citizenship with all the rights every full-blooded American has."

Once again, there was a loud responding roar of "Um gwalla gwalla!"

After his speech, the senator was given a guided tour of the reservation. He saw a high fence and asked what it contained.

The guide said: "That the place where we kept bulls. Now just empty grazing ground. No bulls now."

"Good!" he said, and started to climb over the fence.

His guide warned: "Be careful, senator! You go in there you liable to step in much um gwalla gwalla."

The parish priest couldn't resist the pretty young girl. She was reciting her confession, and it was all too much for him. He told her to come with him to his room. There, he placed his arm around her.

"Did the young man do this to you?" he asked.

"Yes, Father, and worse," the girl replied.

"Hmm," said the priest. He kissed her.

"Did he do this?"

"Yes, Father, and worse," the girl said.

"Did he do this?" the priest asked, and he lifted her skirt and fingered her bush.

"Yes, Father, and worse."

By this time, the priest was thoroughly aroused. He pulled the girl down onto the rug and inserted his penis, breathing heavily as he asked, "Did he manage to do this?"

"Yes, Father, and worse," said the girl.

When the priest had finished with the girl, he asked, "He did this too, and worse? My dear daughter, what worse could he have done?"

"Well," the shy young girl said, "I think, Father, that he's given me gonorrhea."

Little Red Riding Hood was walking through the woods on her way to visit her grandmother, when suddenly a wolf jumped out from behind a tree.

"Ah-ha!" the wolf said, "Now I've got you. And I'm going to eat you!"

"Eat! Eat! Eat!" Little Red Riding Hood said angrily. "Damn it! Doesn't anybody fuck anymore?"

The Frenchman and the Italian were in the woods hunting together when suddenly a voluptuous blonde girl raced across their path, totally nude.

"Would I love to eat that? *Oui, oui!*" the Frenchman said, smacking his lips.

So the Italian shot her.

He had heard that a certain whorehouse in Great Neck, New York, had an unusual reputation for the bizarre. So he drove to the place and, once inside, asked the Madam if she had anything unusual for him to try.

"Things are pretty slow today," she said, "but I do have one number you might enjoy." She went on to describe a New Jersey hen that had been trained to do blow jobs.

"We've got her here, but only for the day."

The visitor could hardly believe it, but he paid the fee and went into a room with the hen. After a frustrating hour of trying to force his cock into the hen's mouth, he figured out that he was dealing with nothing but a plain old chicken. He left.

Thinking about it later, he decided that he had had so much fun trying that he returned the next day and asked the Madam, "Do you have anything new today?"

"Come this way," she said, and led him to a dark room where a group of men were looking through a one-way mirror. He saw that they were watching a girl trying to make it with a dog.

"Wow!" he said to the man standing next to him. "This is really great!"

The man replied, "Man, it ain't nothin'! You shoulda been here yesterday and seen the guy with the chicken."

The recruit had just arrived at a Foreign Legion post in the desert. He asked his corporal what the men did for recreation.

The corporal smiled wisely and said, "You'll see."

The young man was puzzled. "Well, you've got more than a hundred men on this base and I don't see a single woman."

"You'll see," the corporal repeated.

That afternoon, three hundred camels were herded in the corral. At a signal, the men seemed to go wild. They leaped into the corral and began to screw the camels.

The recruit saw the corporal hurrying past him and grabbed his arm. "I see what you mean, but I don't understand," he said. "There must be three hundred of those camels and only about a hundred of us. Why is everybody rushing? Can't a man take his time?"

"What?" exclaimed the corporal, startled. "And get stuck with an ugly one?"

She was wearing a very tight skirt, and when she tried to board the Fifth Avenue bus she found she couldn't lift her leg. She reached back and unzipped her zipper. It didn't seem to do any good, so she reached back and unzipped it again.

Suddenly the man behind her lifted her up and put her on the top step.

"How dare you?" she demanded.

"Well, lady," he said, "by the time you unzipped my fly for the second time I thought we were good friends."

This Chinese laundryman complained to the doctor that he was very constipated. The doctor gave him a prescription for a good physic. "Come to my office in a few days," said the doctor, "and let me know how it works."

A few days later, the Chinaman visited the doctor.

"Have you moved yet?' asked the doctor.

"No, sir, me no moovee, me no moovee."

The doctor scratched his head and then gave the man a prescription for twice as much. Three days later, when the man reported to the doctor again, he said that he still hadn't moved and the doctor gave him a triple dose, and he said, "Come back to see me in two days and let me know just what is happening."

Two days later, the man came back.

"Well," said the doctor, "have you moved yet?"

"No, sir, me no moovee yet. Me moovee tomorrow, though. House full of shit."

This fellow rushed into a crowded tavern on Saturday night. Men and women stood three-deep at the bar. Our man, who felt nature calling strongly, looked about him but couldn't see anything that resembled a john.

He saw a stairway and bounded up the steps to the second floor in his increasingly desperate search. Just as his bowels threatened to erupt, he spotted a one-foot by one-foot hole in the floor. Now, at the end of his control, he decided to take advantage of the hole. He dropped his pants, hunched over it, and did his thing.

Thoroughly relieved and relaxed, he sauntered down the steps to find, to his surprise, that the bar which had been so crowded a few minutes ago, was now empty.

"Hey!" he yelled to the seemingly empty room, "Where is everyone?"

From behind the bar a voice responded, "Where were you when the shit hit the fan?"

A man went to have plastic surgery on his penis. The surgeon examined him and asked, "What happened? '

"Well, doc, I live in a trailer camp," the man explained, "And from where I am I can see this lovely chick next door. She's blonde and she's built like a brick shithouse. She's so horny that every night I see her take a hot dog from the refrigerator and stick it in a hole in the floor of her trailer. Then she gets down and masturbates herself on the hot dog."

"And?" prompted the doctor.

"Well," said the man, "I felt this was a lot of wasted pussy, so one day I got under the trailer and when she put the hot dog in the hole, I removed it and substituted my dick.

"It was a great idea and everything was going real good, too. Then someone knocked at her door, and she jumped off my hot dog and tried to kick it under the stove."

A population control program had been introduced to the island, but the medical men were having trouble getting the women to take their birth control pills. They decided, therefore, to concentrate on teaching the men to wear condoms.

One of the men who came in had had eight children in eight years, and the doctor told him that he absolutely had to wear a sheath. He explained that as long as he wore it his woman could not have another baby.

About a month later, the wife came in and she was pregnant. The doctor got very angry. He called the man in and gave him a long lecture through an interpreter.

He asked the man why he hadn't worn the sheath. The interpreter said, "He swears he did wear it. He never took it off." The doctor shook his head. "In that case, ask him how in hell his wife is pregnant again?"

"He says," said the interpreter, "that after six days he had to take a piss so badly that he cut the end off."

Jordon was young and he was horny. When he arrived at the Foreign Legion post he was disturbed by the total absence of females on the post.

"Jeepers, creepers!" he said to the sergeant. "Don't you fellows have any sex here?"

"Sure we do," said the sergeant. "It's just that we of the French Foreign Legion have to adapt to our environment."

"I don't understand."

"Well," the sergeant explained, "the camels come every Thursday afternoon at three o'clock."

"Camels!" the young man snorted in disgust. "Huh!"

But by Thursday, he couldn't wait. He stood at the edge of the camp scanning the horizon.

At ten to three, he could see a cloud of dust. It grew larger, and then a herd of about twenty camels came thundering into the camp.

Jordon couldn't wait. Grabbing the first one by the bridle, he quickly began to fuck it.

The sergeant ran up to him. "Private Jordon, what in hell are you doing?"

"Christ, sergeant, it's easy enough to see!"

"No, no, you fool! The camels come to take us to town so we can get the girls!"

Jim Buckley went to a farm to visit his country cousin. He went into the barn to watch the country cousin attach the udders of a cow to the milking machine. The machine went up and down and milk poured out.

Buckley was fascinated. As soon as his country cousin left the barn on some errand, he decided to attach the machine to his penis to see how it would feel.

Two hours later, the country cousin returned to find Buckley lying on the floor and moaning, "Ohhhhhh. Let me out! Let me out!"

"Land's sake," the country cousin exclaimed. "What's goin' on?"

"Can't you see?" Buckley said. "I stuck my prick in your damned machine and turned it on. This is the eighty-seventh time I've come! And I can't seem to turn it off!"

The country cousin scratched his head. "Jim, I'm afraid I can't turn it off either. But don t you worry. We'll feed you and fan you, and the thing's only set for four quarts."

So this elderly couple were sitting in their tiny old water flat on the lower East Side when the husband said, "Doris, we're in bad shape. Inflation has eaten up our Social Security check. The next one isn't due for a week and we've got no money left for food."

"Could I do anything to help?" she asked.

"Yes, ' he said. "I hate to see you do this but it's the only way. You're going to have to go out and hustle."

"Me?" she said. "At the age of sixty-five?"

"It's the only way," he said.

Resigned to the situation, she went out into the warm night.

She came staggering in early the next morning.

"How did you do?" asked the husband.

"Here," she said, "I've got four dollars and ten cents."

"Four dollars and ten cents," he said. "Who gave you the ten cents?"

"Everybody," she said.

Garfield Goldwater made a great deal of money in the men's clothing business in New York. He gave to all the charities, attended all the fancy balls, had his name in Earl Wilson's column twice a week— and still wasn't happy. In fact, he was becoming so depressed that a friend suggested he see a psychiatrist.

The psychiatrist listened and then said: "Look here, Mr. Goldwater. You've made all this money, but your success is meaningless because you don't do anything for pleasure. Isn't there anything at all you've always wanted to do? A childhood fantasy? A juvenile ambition?"

"Well," said Garfield Goldwater a little reluctantly, "when I was a boy I wanted to go into the jungle on a safari. You know, kind of like Tarzan did."

The psychiatrist advised: "If that's what you wanted to do, then do it. Life is short and the grave is deep. Do it, man, and do it now!"

Garfield decided to take the advice. Two days later, he flew to Africa, where he confronted the world's most famous gorilla safari hunter.

Patiently, the safari hunter explained that he'd retired. However, Garfield Goldwater was not easily put off. "Please, Mr. Safari Hunter," he said, "make one more safari. I'll pay anything you ask. I'm a rich man. Money is no object."

The safari hunter was moved. "I've heard of you,"

he said. "I've even worn your suits." He thought awhile. Then he asked: "Do you mean what you said about money being no object?"

"Absolutely," vowed Garfield Goldwater.

"All right, here's the deal. In addition to me, you'll need a Zulu, a dog, and a pigmy with a gun. It will cost you ten thousand dollars."

Garfield Goldwater whistled. "Ten thousand dollars!" he exclaimed. "That's a lot of cabbage."

"Only if you don't have it," the safari hunter reminded him.

So Garfield agreed.

The troupe was rounded up, and on the very next afternoon the safari went out on its first mission. Within an hour, the hunter spotted a gorilla in a tree. Everyone stood by while the Zulu climbed the tree. He shook the branches until the gorilla lost his grip and fell to the ground. The dog immediately jumped on the gorilla and bit his penis, at which point the gorilla fainted. A net was slung over him and Garfield had his first gorilla.

He was very pleased. But that night in his tent, Garfield Goldwater thought again about the fee. He went to the safari hunter's tent and awakened him. "I hate to bother you at this hour," he said, "because first, you've done a great job, and second, I'm happy about the gorilla, but third, I think you're taking advantage of me. Ten thousand..."

The safari hunter shrugged. "Mr. Goldwater, a deal is a deal."

"I can understand," said Garfield, "the need for the Zulu and the dog. But why do we need the pigmy with the gun? You're padding the bill a little, old man."

There was no response. The safari hunter had fallen asleep.

The next afternoon, they went out and spotted a larger gorilla in a tree. The Zulu climbed the tree and shook the branches until the gorilla lost his grip and fell to the ground. The dog jumped on the gorilla and bit him on the penis; the gorilla fainted and the safari hunter threw a net over him.

Again Garfield was impressed. But again he began to stew about the high fee. He went to the safari hunter's tent and said: "I want a showdown. I want you to get rid of the pigmy with the gun and reduce my bill."

"Mr. Goldwater," said the safari hunter, "you made a deal. A deal is a deal and that's the deal."

Distraught, Garfield Goldwater returned to his tent. He tried to dream of suits made by Angelo in Rome and ice cream sundaes at Bishoff's in Teaneck, New Jersey, but always his thoughts returned to the ten-thousand-dollar fee and the pigmy with the gun.

The next day, the safari went out, and now it was Garfield Goldwater himself who spotted the gorilla. This time it was a very large one. The Zulu climbed the tree and shook the branches. The Zulu and the gorilla confronted each other, and the two began to wrestle. Suddenly, the gorilla threw the man.

As the Zulu came tumbling down to the ground, he screamed to the pigmy: "Shoot the dog! Shoot the dog!"

Muza Dai Boo, an Arab merchant, was in the marketplace one day when he felt terrible cramps. He just couldn't control himself, and let out a long, loud fart.

People stared at him from all sides. Mortally embarrassed, he ran back to his home, packed his few belongings and journeyed far away. For years he traveled from town to town, but always avoided his home town.

At last, an old and weary man, he decided to return. He had grown a long beard and his face had aged enough so that he was sure he would not be recognized. His heart longed for the old familiar streets.

Once in town, he went directly to the marketplace. There, to his surprise, he saw that the street had been paved. He turned to the man nearest him and said, "My friend, how smooth this street is. When, by the grave of Allah, was it so neatly paved?

"Oh, that," said the man. "That was done three years, four months and two days after Muza Dai Boo farted in the marketplace."

The eighty-eight-year-old millionaire married a fourteen-year-old country girl. He was quite content, but after a few weeks she told him that she was going to leave him if she didn't get some fucking real soon.

He had his chauffeured limousine take him to a high-priced specialist who studied him and then gave him a shot of spermatozoa. "Now look," the doctor said, "The only way you're going to get it hard is to say 'beep,' and then to get it soft again, you say 'beep beep.'"

"How marvelous," the old man said.

"Yes, but I must warn you," the doctor said, "it's only going to work three times before you die."

On his way home, the old man decided he wasn't going to live through three of them anyway, so he decided to waste one trying it out.

"Beep!" he said.

Immediately, his penis got hard.

Satisfied, he said "beep, beep," and his penis got soft again. He chucked with delight and anticipation.

At that moment, a little yellow Volkswagen pulled past his limousine and went "beep," and the car in the opposite lane responded with "beep beep."

Alert to his jeopardy, the old man instructed his chauffeur to "speed it up." He raced into the house as fast as he could for his last great fuck. "Honey," he shouted at her, "don't ask any questions. Just drop your clothes and hop into bed."

Caught up in his excitement, she did. He undressed nervously and hurried in after her. Just as he was climbing into the bed, he said "beep," and his penis leaped to erection.

He was just starting to put it in when his tender young wife said, "What's all this 'beep beep' shit?"

The teacher walked into the classroom to find words like "cunt" and "cock" scrawled all over the blackboard.

"Children," she said, addressing the classroom. "You are much too young to use vile language like that. Now, we're all going to close our eyes and count up to fifty. Then, while our eyes are closed, I want the little boy or girl who wrote those words on the board to tiptoe up and erase them."

At the signal, the teacher and the children all closed their eyes. Then the teacher counted out loud, very slowly.

When she reached fifty, she said, "All right. Everybody open their eyes."

All eyes went to the blackboard.

None of the words were erased. But below them was the message: "Fuck you, teacher. The Phantom strikes again!"

Silas and Sally were out in the cornfield happily fucking away. It had rained that morning and there was lots of mud on the ground, and they found themselves sliding around a bit in the mud.

"Say, honey, is my cock in you or in the mud?" Silas asked.

Sally felt around and said, "Why, Silas, it's in the mud!"

"Well, put it back in you," he said.

After awhile, Silas asked again, "Honey, is it in you or in the mud?"

"In me, honey. In me," Sally cooed happily.

"Well, would you mind putting it back in the mud?"

The teacher told the students that they were going to play a game.

"I've got something behind my back and I'm going to describe it and you guess what it is," she said.

"I'm holding something round and red. Can someone guess?"

"'An apple?" little Herbie said.

"No," said the teacher, "but it shows you were thinking. It's a cherry. Now I'm holding something round and orange. Can you tell me what it is?"

"An orange?" little Herbie said.

"No," said the teacher, "but it shows you were thinking. It's a peach."

Herbie raised his hand. "Teacher, can I play the game too?"

The teacher said yes, and Herbie went to the back of the room, faced the rear and said, "Teacher, I'm holding something about two inches long with a red tip."

The teacher said, "Herbie!"

"No," said little Herbie, "but it shows you were thinking. It's a match."

It happened in Paris in the spring. On a sunny day in May, a Chinaman picked up a whore on the Champs Elysées and took her to the Meurice Hotel.

They opened the windows and the breeze blew in and everything seemed beautiful. The Chinaman got into bed with the whore. He fucked her for awhile and then said, *"Pardonnez-moi, Mademoiselle, je suis fatigué."*

So saying, he went to the window and took a deep breath. Then he went under the bed, came out the other side, and jumped into bed to screw again.

After awhile, he got up saying, *"Pardonnez-moi, Mademoiselle, je suis fatigué."* Again he went to the window, took a deep breath, rolled under the bed and came out the other side.

The sixth time this happened, the whore had become very tired too. Getting out of bed, she said, *"Pardonnez-moi, Monsieur, je suis fatigué."*

She went to the open window, took a deep breath, and looked under the bed. She found four other Chinamen there.

One Friday afternoon, Harold's boss told him that he'd have to work overtime that day. That was okay with Harold except that he had no way of letting his wife know he'd be late coming home, since they had just moved into a new little house in the suburbs and didn't have a phone yet.

"Since I'm passing that way, I'll tell her," the boss volunteered.

A few hours later, the boss arrived at the cottage and rang the doorbell. Harold's wife came to the door wearing a see-through wraparound. The boss couldn't take his eyes off her body.

"Yes?" she said.

"I'm Harold's boss," Harold's boss said. "He's working overtime and asked me to tell you he'll be home late."

"Thank you," she said.

"How about going upstairs for some fucking?"

Harold's wife felt her cheeks flush to an angry red. "How dare you!"

The boss shrugged. "Supposing I give you fifty dollars?"

"Absolutely not! Why, I never heard such nerve. . . ."

"One hundred dollars?"

"Uh . . . no."

"One hundred and fifty?"

"I don't think that would be right, do you?"

At this point, the boss purred, "Listen, honey, Harold isn't gonna know. It's an easy way to make a hundred and fifty bucks and we'll just spend a little time together."

She nodded, took him by the hand, and led him upstairs to the bed where they had fun and games for an hour.

That night, when Harold came home, he asked, "Did the boss come by to tell you I'd be late?"

"Yes, Harold," the sweet thing said, "he did stop by for a few seconds."

"Good," said Harold. "Then he gave you my salary?"

B enson had been with prostitutes everywhere in the world, but in Hong Kong he met his undoing. He fucked a very sick Chinese whore and picked up so many venereal diseases that the doctors had difficulty separating and identifying them all.

He went to a prominent gynecologist in the American quarter who examined him and shook his head. "Bad news, Benson. You must have immediate surgery and we've got to cut your penis off."

Benson went into traumatic shock at the prognosis. Gathering himself together, he went across the street to another American doctor. There he was told the same thing.

He went out into the street in a daze. Stumbling along, he found himself in the Chinese quarter, where he saw a sign identifying the office of a Chinese surgeon.

Deciding to have one more medical opinion, Benson went in. He told the Chinese doctor that he'd been to two American doctors and both of them wanted to perform immediate surgery to cut off his cock.

The Chinese surgeon examined Benson's penis. He consulted large medical books. Then he examined it again.

"Is there any hope, doc?" Benson asked, plaintively.

"Sure is hope!" the doctor said. "I make complete

examination. I know just what's wrong. You play with Chinese girl, but she very sick. You make mistake and go to American doctor. Trouble with American doctors, they always think money, money, money."

Benson brightened up. "You mean I don't need surgery? My penis doesn't have to be cut off?"

"Forget what they say. Go home," the Chinese doctor repeated. "No surgery. Go home. Wait two, maybe three weeks. Pecker fall off all by himself."

A man took his wife to a Broadway show. During the first act intermission, he had to urinate in the worst way. He hurried to the back of the theatre and searched in vain for the men's room.

At last he came upon a fountain surrounded by pretty foliage. He realized that he had wandered backstage. Noting that no one was around, and in desperation, he opened his pants and pissed into the fountain.

He had difficulty finding his way back to the auditorium, and by the time he sat down next to his wife, the curtain was up and actors were moving about on the stage.

"Did I miss much of the second act?" he whispered.

"Miss it?" she said, "You were in it!"

The man was dining in a very swank restaurant in New York City. When the elderly waiter brought the consommé the customer saw that his thumb was deep in the soup bowl.

Next, the waiter served *steak Diane*, and now his thumb was deep in the gravy. The customer held his tongue. This was, after all, one of New York's finest restaurants.

Finally, for dessert, the waiter brought out *coupe marron*. This time his finger was not in the ice cream.

The customer could contain himself no longer. "Sir," he said to the waiter, "would you tell me why you put your finger in the consommé and the steak gravy, but not in the *coupe marron*?"

The waiter stared coldly at him for a moment, and then replied, "Simple, my good man. I have a bad case of arthritis and warm things relieve the pain in my thumb."

The customer became very angry. "You son-of-a-bitch!" he said, "Putting your thumb in my food! You should take that thumb and ram it up your ass!"

The waiter looked at him dourly and said, "That's what I do in the kitchen."

Do you know the difference between a cocksucker and a corned beef sandwich?

No.

Good. Come over tomorrow for lunch.

The Japanese-American was a long-time customer at this Greek restaurant because he had discovered that they made especially tasty fried rice. Each evening he'd come in he would order "flied lice."

This always caused the Greek restaurant owner to nearly roll on the floor with laughter. Sometimes he'd have two or three friends stand nearby just to hear the Japanese customer order his "flied lice."

Eventually, the customer's pride was so hurt that he took a special diction lesson just to be able to say "fried rice" correctly.

The next time he went to the restaurant, he said very plainly, "Fried rice, please."

Unable to believe his ears, the Greek restaurant owner said, "Sir, would you repeat that?"

The Japanese-American replied: "You heard what I said, you fluckin Gleek!"

The Israeli army unit was crossing the desert and most of the men were on camels. Lt. Smith had a very stubborn camel, and finally it stopped dead in its tracks and refused to move another step.

The rest of the unit moved on, leaving Smith along with his mulish camel.

Smith sat on the camel for three hours. He kicked the camel. He pleaded with the camel. He shouted curses at the camel. But the camel wouldn't move.

He dismounted, and was standing disconsolately at its side when a woman soldier drove up in a jeep. She asked Lt. Smith what the trouble was, and he explained the camel wouldn't budge.

"Oh, I can fix that," she said, jumping out of her jeep. She reached down and put her hand under the camel's belly. The camel jumped up and down, up again, and then suddenly raced away at the rate of half a mile a minute.

Lt. Smith was astounded. "What did you do, lady? What's the trick?"

"It's simple, Lieutenant. I just tickled his balls."

"Well, lady, you'd better tickle mine too, and quickly, because I've got to catch that camel!"

A man was asked by his wife to buy a live chicken for a special dinner. He bought the chicken and was on his way home when he remembered that he didn't have his house key and his wife wouldn't be there for a few hours.

He decided to pass the time by going to a movie. In order to get into the cinema, he stuffed the chicken into his trousers.

He sat down and began watching the movie. It fascinated him so that he didn't notice the chicken sticking its head through his fly.

Two women were sitting next to him, and one of them nudged the other. "Look," she said, "look at that thing there sticking out of the man's pants."

The other replied, "If you've seen one, you've seen them all."

The first one said, "Yes, but this one is eating my popcorn!"

Three nuns were walking along the street and one was describing with her hands the tremendous grapefruit she'd seen in Florida.

The second one, also with her hands, described the huge bananas she'd seen in Jamaica.

The third nun, a little deaf, asked, "Father who?"

So there were these two blacks from a southern town and they wanted women desperately but couldn't find any. They were driving along the country road when they spotted a pig. One of them jumped out, scooped up the pig and stuck it on the seat between them.

They continued to chug along in their 1969 Ford when a police siren suddenly sounded behind them. A glance at the rear view mirror showed them that a police car was in hot pursuit. They pulled over to the side. Not wanting to be caught with a stolen pig, they tossed a blanket over it.

The officer came up to the side of their car. "What are you up to?" he asked.

"We were just out looking for women," one of the lads replied truthfully.

Suddenly the pig stuck its face through the folds of the blanket.

The cop stared, shook his head sadly, and said, "Lady, can you tell me what a nice Southern girl like you is doing with these two Blacks?"

A man was standing on a train platform seeing the train off and he observed someone near him shouting at one of the departing passengers, "Goodbye. Your wife was a great lay! Your wife was a great lay!"

He was stunned.

After the train pulled away, he walked over to the man who'd done the shouting, and asked, "Did I hear you correctly? Did you tell that man his wife was a great lay?"

The other man shrugged his shoulders. "It isn't really true," he said, "but I don't want to hurt his feelings."

The little boy was sitting on the curb crying and an old man who was passing by came over to him.

"What's the matter, little boy?" he asked. "Why are you crying?"

The little boy said, "I'm crying because I can't do what the big boys do."

The old man sat down on the curb and cried too.

Some Americans were touring the marketplace and one of them saw a man on the ground brushing his camel.

"Excuse me, sir," the American said. "Do you know the time?"

The Arab looked at the American. Then he reached over and held the camel's balls, moving them slightly.

"Ten after two," he said, at last.

"My word!" said the American. He caught up to his tour group and insisted some of the others return with him. "You've never seen anything like this!" he promised.

The group went back with him. Again he asked for the time. Again the Arab camel driver reached for the camel's balls. He seemed to be weighing them as he moved them to and fro. Finally, he announced: "Twenty-one minutes past two."

The others were amazed. They went on their way, but the original discoverer of the miracle time-teller remained. He leaned over. "Listen," he confided to the Arab. "I'd give anything to know how you do that. I'll give you twenty American dollars if you show me how you tell the time."

The Arab camel driver thought for a moment, and then nodded. Pocketing the twenty-dollar bill, he beckoned for the American to kneel down where he was.

Then he took the camel's balls and gently moved them to the side, out of the way.

"Do you see that clock over there?" he asked.

He was a junior bank executive and he had swindled one hundred thousand dollars from his bank—all of which he'd lost at the races. The bank examiners were coming the next day, and when he confessed the whole thing to his wife, she packed her bags and left him. Totally despondent, he walked to a nearby bridge and stood at the edge of it about to jump off and end it all.

Suddenly a voice called, "Young man, don't do that! There is no need to end your life! I'm a witch and I can help you!"

"I doubt it," he said sadly, "I've stolen a hundred thousand dollars from the bank, for which I'll probably be arrested tomorrow, and my wife has left me."

"Young man, witches can do anything," she said. "I'm going to perform a witch miracle." She said, "*Alakazam!* the hundred thousand dollars has been replaced and there's another hundred thousand in your safe deposit box! *Alakazam!* Your wife is back home again!"

He looked at her in disbelief, "Is this all true?" he asked.

"Of course," she said, "but to keep it true you must do one thing."

"Anything!" he said, "Anything!"

"You must take me to a motel and have sexual intercourse with me."

He stared at her. She was an ugly old crone, dressed in rags. Nevertheless, he agreed to her terms. He took her to a motel and screwed her all night. In the morning, as he was getting dressed and combing his hair in front of the mirror, she lay on the bed watching silently. Finally, she asked, "Sonny, how old are you?"

"I'm thirty-two," he said.

"Tell me something, then," she said. "Aren't you a little too old to believe in witches?"

It was his wedding night and the minister finished undressing in the bathroom and walked into the bedroom. He was surprised to see that his bride had already slipped between the bed sheets.

"My dear," he said, "I thought I would find you on your knees."

She said, "Well, honey, I can do it that way too, but it gives me the hiccoughs."

The newly-married Italian couple came home to Brooklyn from their honeymoon and moved into the upstairs apartment they'd rented from the groom's parents.

That night, the father of the groom was awakened from his deep sleep by his wife nudging him by hitting his stomach with her elbow. "Tony, listen!" she whispered.

He listened. Upstairs, the bed was creaking in rhythm.

The wife said, "Come on, Tony!" So Tony rolled on top of her and fucked her.

He was trying to fall back to sleep when, fifteen minutes later, the same sounds were heard. The wife said, "Tony! Listen to them! Come on, Tony!"

Once again, Tony got on top of her and fucked her.

A short time later, the bedsprings upstairs began to squeak again. And again the wife nudged her husband. "Tony, listen!" At this, Tony leaped from the bed, grabbed a broom, and banged the handle against the ceiling as he shouted, "Hey, kids, cut it out! You're killing your old man!"

So this husband from Roslyn Heights, Long Island, kissed his wife goodbye and got into his Cadillac to drive to work in New York City. He'd gone about a mile when he remembered that he'd left something in the bedroom. So he turned the car around and drove back home.

When he walked into the bedroom, there was his wife, lying totally nude on the bed and the milkman standing totally nude beside her.

The milkman promptly went into a squatting position on the rug and said, "I'm glad you're here, Mr. Jones, because I was just telling your wife that if she doesn't pay the milk bill, I'm gonna shit all over the floor."

A man who was very depressed met his friend, Jerry J., who was a very sharp thinker.

"What's the matter?" Jerry J. asked.

"I'm despondent. I can't adjust to the fact that I've got three balls."

"Three balls?" said sharp Jerry. "Kid, we can make a fortune together!"

"How?" asked the other fellow, brightening up.

"We'll go to bar after bar and bet everybody around that between you and the bartender you've got five balls! It can't miss!"

"Let's go," said the man.

So they went into the first bar, and Jerry J. made friends with the strangers at the bar. Then he made the announcement: "I'll bet anybody in the place that between my friend here and the bartender they've got five balls."

Nearly everyone rushed forward to cover the bet.

Jerry looked at the bartender who was shaking his head.

"You don't mind being part of the wager, do you?" Jerry asked.

"Not at all," the bartender said. "I'm very impressed."

"How do you mean?" Jerry asked.

"Well, up to now I've never met a man with four balls. I've only got one."

A young farm boy from Arkansas was sent to New York by his father to learn the undertaking business under the tutelage of the great Frank E. Campbell.

Some months later, the father visited his son in the big city. "Tell me," he said, "have you learned much?"

"Oh sure, Dad," said the son. I've learned a lot. And it's been very interesting."

"What was the most interesting thing you learned?"

The son thought for a minute and then said, "Well, we did have one wild experience that taught me a lesson."

"What was that?"

"Well," said the son, "one day we got this phone call from the Taft Hotel. It seems that the housekeeper had checked one of the rooms and she discovered that a man and woman had died in their sleep on the bed and completely naked."

"Wow!" said the father. "What did Mr. Campbell do?"

"Well, he put on his tuxedo and he had me put on my tuxedo. Then we were driven in one of his limousines to the Taft Hotel. The manager took us to the desk clerk who gave us the room number. Then the manager rode up with us in the elevator. We were silent because Mr. Campbell always believed in doing things with great dignity."

"How marvelous!" exclaimed the father. "Then what happened?"

"Well, we came to this room. Mr. Campbell pushed the door open with his gold tipped cane. He, the manager, and I walked in quietly. Sure enough, there on the bed was this naked couple lying on their backs."

"And then what happened?" asked the father.

"Well, Mr. Campbell saw an immediate problem. The man had a large erection."

"And then what happened?" asked the father.

"Mr. Campbell, as usual, was up to the situation. He swung his gold-tipped cane and very stylishly whacked the penis."

"And then what happened?" asked the father.

"Well, Dad," said the son, "all hell broke loose. You see, we were in the wrong room!"

The Mother Superior in the convent school was chatting with her young charges and she asked them what they wanted to be when they grew up.

A twelve-year-old said, "I want to be a prostitute."

The Mother Superior fainted dead away on the spot. When they revived her, she raised her head from the ground and gasped, "What—did—you—say—?"

The young girl shrugged. "I said I want to be a prostitute."

"A prostitute!" the Mother Superior said, "Oh, praise sweet Jesus! And I thought you said you wanted to be a Protestant."

Little Jimmy had become a real nuisance while the men tried to concentrate on their Saturday afternoon poker game. His father tried in every way he could to get Jimmy to occupy himself, but the youngster insisted on running back and forth behind the players and calling out the cards they held.

The players became so annoyed that they threatened to quit the game. At this point, the boy's uncle stood up, took Jimmy by the hand, and led him out of the room. The uncle returned in a short time without Jimmy and without comment, and the game resumed.

For the balance of the afternoon, there was no trouble from Jimmy. After the game had ended and the players were settling their wins and losses, one of the men asked Jimmy's uncle, "What in the world did you do to Jimmy?"

"Not much," the boy's uncle replied. "I showed him how to jerk off."

The bridegroom carried his bride over the threshold and into the honeymoon suite. They had taken off all their clothes, when suddenly the sweet young thing began to tremble.

"What's the matter, honey?" he asked in a concerned voice.

She was now shivering all over. "I've got an attack of St. Vitus Dance," she said.

The groom thought about it for a minute, then picked up the hotel phone and called the bell captain for help.

Four bellboys came rushing into the room.

"Quick! You grab her arms," the young man shouted to two of them. To the other two, he directed, "Grab her legs and hold her tight."

He leaped into the bed on top of her, inserted his penis into her, and then shouted to the straining bellboys, "Okay, fellows, let her go!"

A Frenchman who was leaving his home in Paris for a few weeks confided in his friend, Pierre: "I always hate to leave the city. When I'm away, I just don't know what my wife is doing. There's always the doubt, always the doubt."

Pierre said, "Charles, I'll tell you what. Because we're such good friends, I'll keep an eye on her every evening that you're gone."

"Would you do that for me?" Charles said, obviously delighted and relieved. He kissed Pierre on both cheeks. "You understand, dear friend, that I know I should trust my wife. It's just that there's always the doubt, always the doubt."

"Have no fear, Pierre will be there," the friend said.

Three weeks later, Charles returned to Paris and the two men met.

"Charles, I'm afraid I have bad news for you," Pierre said.

"Well?"

"The very first night you were gone, I watched this man go to your house. Your wife opened the door and kissed and hugged him. He fondled her breast. He rubbed her crotch. Then they closed the door to go upstairs. Never daunted, I climbed the tree outside your house and I observed them closely from one of its branches."

"And so—?" said Charles.

"Well, first they took off all their clothes. Incidentally, dear friend, your wife has a lovely body."

"She does, indeed," said Charles thoughtfully. "What happened then?"

"Then?" Pierre shook his head sorrowfully. "Then is when they turned out the lights. I could see nothing. I could learn nothing more."

Charles sighed a deep sigh. "So you see how it is, my friend? Always the doubt, always the doubt."

Two factory workers were at their lathes and one of them said, "Listen, are you going to the hockey game tomorrow night? You know, it's the big game. The Rangers are playing Montreal."

"Naw," said the other one, "my wife won't let me go."

"You're a fool. There's nothing to it."

"What do you mean?"

"Well, an hour before the game you simply pick her up, carry her to the bed, fling her on the bed, tear off her clothes, fuck her, and say, 'I'm going to the hockey game'!"

The following Monday, the two men met at work and the first one said, "What happened? I didn't see you at the game. Didn't you do what I suggested?"

The second man said: "I'll tell you how it was. An hour before the game, I picked up the wife, carried her to the bedroom, and flung her onto the bed."

"Yes?"

"And then, just as I was pulling off her panties and opening my fly, I thought to myself, what the hell, Montreal hasn't been playing that well lately."

The judge came home and found his wife in bed with his very best friend.

"Hey, what do you think you're doing?"

"See," the wife said to the man beside her, "I told you he was stupid."

This seedy looking girl walked into a seedy looking bar. A couple of seeding looking customers stood at the other end.

"Gimme a Rheingold," she said.

She took the glass of beer and swallowed it with one gulp. Then she fell to the floor in a dead faint.

"Come, give me a hand," the bartender called. The two men helped the bartender carry her into the back room. One of the men glanced around and said, "Listen. Nobody'll know. How about we all give her a quick fuck?"

They did just that. An hour or so later, she came to and said, "Where am I? What time is it? I've got to get home." And out she went.

Next afternoon, there were six men hanging around the bar when the same girl came in, walked up to the bartender and said, "Gimme a Rheingold."

She drank it down in one gulp and then fell to the floor in a dead faint.

The men carried her to the back room and the fucking performance was repeated, except that now there were seven, including the bartender.

The next day when she came in, there were twenty-four men, all waiting around.

"Gimme a Rheingold," she said. She swallowed it in one gulp, fell to the floor in a dead faint, and was carried to the back room, where all twenty-four men partook of her.

When she arrived on the fourth day, the word had really gotten around, and there were more than seventy men in the bar, waiting eagerly with lustful eyes and eager cocks. As the walked up to the bar, the bartender pushed a glass of beer toward her.

"You want your Rheingold, Miss?" she said.

"No," she said. "You better give me a Schlitz. That Rheingold gives me a pain in the cunt."

He was very wealthy and very old—in fact, he was about to celebrate his eighty-third birthday. He went to the doctor for a checkup. The doctor gave him a thorough going-over, and then said, "For a man who's about to be eighty-three, you're in marvelous shape. But why a physical just a day before your birthday?"

The wealthy old man explained that that very afternoon he was going to marry an eighteen-year-old girl.

The doctor tried with a great deal of effort to dissuade him. "I'm goin' ahead with it no matter what," the old man said. "Got any other suggestions, Doc?"

"Just one. If you want a really peaceful marriage, I suggest that you take in a boarder."

The old man thought about it and said that it sounded like a good idea.

The next time the doctor met the old man it was at a fund-raising affair, half a year later. The old man came up to him and said, "Doctor, congratulate me! My wife's pregnant!"

The doctor tried to maintain his poise, and said, "Well, so at least you followed my good advice and took in a boarder."

"Oh, sure," said the old man, with a wicked grin, "and the boarder's pregnant as well!"

Once upon a time there was a sperm named Stanley who lived inside a famous movie actor. Stanley was a very healthy sperm. He'd do push-ups and somersaults and limber himself up all the time, while the other sperm just lay around on their fat asses not doing a thing.

One day, one of them became curious enough to ask Stanley why he exercised all day.

Stanley said, "Look, pal, only one sperm gets a woman pregnant and when the right time comes, I am going to be that one."

A few days later, they all felt themselves getting hotter and hotter, and they knew that it was getting to be their time to go. They were released abruptly and, sure enough, there was Stanley swimming far ahead of all the others.

All of a sudden, Stanley stopped, turned around, and began to swim back with all his might. "Go back! Go back!" he screamed. "It's a blow job!"

He was on his way home when he came upon a woman crying hysterically. "What's the matter, lady?" he asked.

She could only sob, "Schultz is dead. Schultz is dead!"

He shook his head and continued walking. Suddenly he came upon another woman sobbing, "Schultz is dead, Schultz is dead!"

He couldn't get over it because soon he came upon another woman crying the same thing. He had never seen so many unhappy women. And then he came upon a scene that caused him to stop. A trolley car had run over a man and had cut him into pieces. There, on the pavement next to the body, was this foot-and-a-half-long penis, and a half-dozen women were standing around crying hysterically, "Schultz is dead. Schultz is dead!"

When he arrived home, he greeted his wife with, "I just saw the damndest thing. A trolley car ran over a man and cut off his cock, and would you believe it, the cock was a foot and a half long."

"Oh my God!" the wife screamed, "Schultz is dead. Schultz is dead!"

Marilyn had a parrot for a pet, but the parrot would embarrass her whenever she came into the apartment with a man. He would shout all kinds of obscenities, always leading off with "Somebody's gonna get it tonight! Somebody's gonna get it tonight!"

In desperation, Marilyn went to her local pet shop and explained her parrot problem to the pet shop proprietor.

"What you need," he said, "is a female parrot too. I don't have one on hand, but I'll order one. Meanwhile, you could borrow this female owl until the female parrot arrives."

Marilyn took the owl home and put it near her parrot. It was immediately obvious that the parrot didn't care for the owl. He glared at it.

The night, Marilyn wasn't her usual nervous self as she opened the door to bring her gentleman friend in for a nightcap. Then suddenly she heard the parrot screech and she knew that things hadn't changed.

"Somebody's gonna get it tonight! Somebody's gonna get it tonight!" the parrot said.

The owl said, "Whooo? Whooo?

And the parrot said, "Not you, you big-eyed son-of-a-bitch!"

The
World's Best
Football
Jokes

'It's a funny old game, football,' as the captain said to the manager after his team had been trounced 6—0 in an important relegation match.

To which the manager replied grimly, 'Yes – but it isn't meant to be!'

What is football? It has been described as a game with twenty-two players, two linesmen and 20,000 referees.

One of the most famous footballers of all time is the legendary Stanley Matthews, who played for Blackpool and Stoke City at outside-right. It was said of him that he was so fast that when he went to bed at night, he could turn out the light at the bedroom door and be under the blankets before the room got dark.

A Scottish captain once lent the referee a coin for the toss and demanded his whistle as security.

Why do Pakistanis make very poor footballers? Every time you give them a corner they open a shop on it.

A desperate manager, whose team had lost fourteen consecutive games, rang a colleague for advice on training methods.

'I'll tell you what you should do,' said his friend. 'Take the team out on a six-mile run every day.'

'What's the point of that?' asked the manager.

'Today's Monday,' was the reply. 'By Saturday, they'll be thirty-six miles away and you can forget all about them!'

The manager of a club way down at the bottom of the Fourth Division placed eleven dustbins in formation on the pitch and had his team practise dribbling around them and passing between them before shooting for goal. After just one session he had to abandon this method of training for reasons of team morale: the dustbins won 6—0.

A match between two non-League teams took place last winter in the North of England. It had been raining heavily all week and the ground resembled a swamp. However, the referee ruled that play was possible and tossed the coin to determine ends. The visiting captain won the toss and, after a moment's thought, said, 'OK – we'll take the shallow end!'

The following instruction recently appeared on the noticeboard of a large car factory in Cowley: ALL APPLICATIONS FOR LEAVE OF ABSENCE FOR FAMILY BEREAVEMENTS, SICKNESS, JURY DUTY, ETC., MUST BE HANDED IN TO THE PERSONNEL MANAGER NO LATER THAN 6 P.M. ON THE DAY PRECEDING THE MATCH.

A goalkeeper had had a particularly bad season and announced that he was retiring from professional football. In a television interview he was asked his reasons for quitting the game. 'Well, basically,' he said, 'it's a question of illness and fatigue.'

'Can you be more specific?' asked the interviewer.

'Well,' said the player, 'specifically the fans are sick and tired of me.'

Over breakfast one morning, a little boy kept staring intently at his grandfather. 'Is anything the matter, son?' the old man asked.

'No, Gramps. I was just wondering what position you play in the football team.'

'What are you talking about?' laughed Gramps. 'I'm far too old to play football.'

'Oh,' said the little boy. 'It's just that Dad said that when you kicked off, we'd be able to afford a new car.'

In a particularly rough tackle, a player was knocked unconscious. A first-aid man ran over and began to sprinkle water in his face and fan him with a towel. Slowly the player recovered consciousness and said groggily, 'How the hell do they expect us to play in all this wind and rain?'

One Friday afternoon, late last season, a leading member of a big First Division club was tragically knocked down and killed by a hit-and-run driver. One of the reserves, seeing a chance to get a game at last, approached the coach and asked, 'Do you think I could take his place, boss?'

'That's a good idea,' replied the coach. 'I'll see if I can arrange it with the undertaker.'

A football widow decided to take an interest in the game in order to share her husband's pastime. One Saturday afternoon she accompanied him to the local match. It was a good game: plenty of open play, good attacking movements and strong defence. She was enjoying the game when suddenly all the players except one froze and stood like statues. The active player grabbed the ball and shoved it up his jersey.

Then he too remained motionless. The woman looked at the referee to see what action he was going to take, but he too was in a statue-like position.

'Whatever are they doing?' she asked.

'Oh, they're posing for the "Spot-the-Ball" competition,' replied her husband.

An American visitor to England watched his very first football match and was struck by the differences between English and American football. After the match he fell into conversation with one of the English players and remarked, 'You know, over in the States, our players wear thick protective clothing. You guys must be frozen stiff in those light clothes.'

'It's not so bad,' said the Englishman. 'Sometimes the ground is covered in snow.'

'You don't say!' exclaimed the American. 'What do you do about the balls? Paint them red?'

'Oh, no,' said the player. 'We just wear an extra pair of shorts.'

A Fourth Division coach was addressing his team during a training session. 'Now, lads,' he said, 'over the last few months, I've given you a lot of tips and advice on passing, dribbling, kicking and defensive play.' The team nodded appreciately. 'Well, you can forget it all,' said the coach, 'because we've just sold the bloody lot of you!'

A well-known footballer and his wife recently decided to take a holiday at a nudist camp. He was asked to referee the camp football match but, surprisingly, he declined the offer. 'Why did you refuse to referee that match?' asked his wife.

'I wasn't too happy about where I had to carry the spare whistle,' replied the husband.

There was once a match in Liverpool between Anglican vicars and Roman Catholic priests. Early in the game the Catholics were awarded a penalty. Father Flanagan placed the ball carefully, took a long run at it, and kicked. The ball sailed high into the air and missed the goal by miles. Father Flanagan didn't utter a word. He just stood there with a grim expression on his face. The team captain, Monsignor Ryan, came up behind him and said reprovingly, 'Father, that is the most profane silence I have ever heard!'

It was the last game of the season. Mathieson had been with the team from the start but he was such a slow and clumsy player that never once had he actually been allowed to play, but had spent all his time on the substitute bench. At this last match, however, there were so many fouls and injuries that every substitute but him had been sent on. With ten minutes to go, yet another player was carried off the field and the coach looked at the substitute bench, his eye finally alighting on Mathieson. Mathieson's face lit up. 'Are you going to send me on, coach?' he asked eagerly.

'No!' snapped the coach. 'Just get out of the way. I'm going to send in the bench!'

The reigning Miss World – from Brazil – was invited to start a charity football match by performing the ceremonial kick-off. After an excellent game, which raised a great deal of money, a dinner was held. During the speeches which followed, Miss World made the evening for all present when, in broken English and with great charm, she said, 'It eez great honour for me to kick off your ball; I will be pleased to come back any time to English football clubs and kick all your balls off.'

Did you hear about the England international player who had a date with a referee's daughter? She penalised him three times – for handling, interference and trying to pull off a jersey.

Referees at Celtic Rangers matches always have a particularly hard time. One poor unfortunate, officiating at his first fixture, was checking in with the team managers before the kick-off. 'Well, that seems to be about everything,' said the Rangers boss. 'Now, if you'd just like to give us the name and address of your next-of-kin, we can start the match.'

A player was being ticked off by the coach for missing a very easy goal-kick. 'All right,' said the player, 'how *should* I have played the shot?'
'Under an assumed name,' snapped the coach.

The football club dance was in full swing when three strangers arrived and demanded admission. 'May I see your tickets, please?' said the club secretary at the door.

'We haven't got any tickets,' said one of the men. 'We're friends of the referee.'

'Get out of here!' said the club secretary. 'Whoever heard of a referee with three friends!'

'When I started as a commentator,' says John Motson, 'I was bombarded by letters from an irate viewer in the north who resented my reference to the colour of shirts which teams were wearing. His point was that he came from a working-class family who could not afford colour television, and was fed up with being told who was in the red shirts or the green shirts, when he had no way of identifying them. Determined to do something to pacify him, I waited for a quiet moment in a match at Roker Park, and then came out with a remark I have never been allowed to forget! "For those watching in black-and-white," I said, "Spurs are in the yellow shirts!" '

John once received a letter from the Race Relations Board when, after a particularly good goal by Watford, he said, 'There's a case of Barnes doing the spade-work for Blissett!' He adds that he didn't intend this remark to come out the way it did – although nobody laughed louder than the black players themselves!

Another well-known television sports commentator, who shall be nameless, was talking to his friends in the pub one night. 'It's amazing,' he said. 'I've been in the business for twenty years and it just occurred to me today that I don't know anything about the game at all!'

'Well, why don't you give it up then?' asked a bystander.

'I can't,' replied the commentator. 'I've become a world authority!'

THE BEST OF 'COLEMANBALLS'

'Their manager, Terry Neil, isn't here today, which suggests he is elsewhere.' (Brian Moore)

'With the very last kick of the game, Bobby McDonald scored with a header.' (Alan Parry)

'Well, it's Ipswich nil, Liverpool two, and if that's the way the score stays then you've got to fancy Liverpool to win.' (Peter Jones)

'Bolton are on the crest of a slump.' (Anon)

'You couldn't have counted the number of moves Alan Ball made . . . I counted four and possibly five.' (John Motson)

'When one team scores early in the game, it often takes an early lead.' (Pat Marsden)

'And Meade had a hat-trick. He scored two goals.' (Richard Whitmore)

'I am a firm believer that if you score one goal, the other team have to score two to win.' (Howard Wilkinson)

'Ian Rush unleashed his left foot and it hit the back of the net.' (Mike England)

'It will be a shame if either side lose. And that applies to both sides.' (Jock Brown)

'It was a good match which could have gone either way and very nearly did.' (Jim Sherwin)

'He had an eternity to play that ball, but he took too long over it.' (Martin Tyler)

'Everything in our favour was against us.' (Danny Blanch-flower)

'Nearly all the Brazilian players are wearing yellow shirts. It's a fabulous kaleidoscope of colour.' (John Motson)

'And so they have not been able to improve on their hundred percent record.' (Sports Roundup)

The Oxford and Cambridge University student teams were due to play when one of the Oxford men had to drop out at short notice. 'Why don't we use Johnson, the head porter at Balliol?' suggested the Oxford captain to the selection committee. 'I've seen him play in a local amateur team and he's a brilliant striker – absolutely unstoppable. We can get him a set of colours and as long as he doesn't speak to anyone, we should be able to get away with it.'

The committee thought this might be a little unethical but in desperation they agreed to the plan. They rigged out the Balliol porter and put him on the left wing. He was, as the Oxford captain had said, unstoppable, and they beat Cambridge 9—1, Johnson having scored eight of the goals single-handed.

Afterwards in the bar, the Cambridge captain approached Johnson and said sportingly, 'Well done, old boy! A magnificent effort! By the way, what are you studying at Balliol?'

The porter thought for a moment, then said brightly, 'Sums!'

One of the lesser-known stories in Greek mythology tells of a classic football match on Mount Olympus between the Gods and the Mortals. The Gods trounced the Mortals 8—0 and attributed their victory to the brilliance of their new centaur-forward.

A First Division reserves team recently played against a side made up of long-term prisoners from Strangeways. (The Strangeways team were playing at home, of course!) The game had only been in progress for about ten minutes when the referee noticed that the prison team were fielding twelve men. Blowing his whistle angrily, he called the Strangeways captain over and said, 'What the hell's the idea of having twelve men on the field? Don't you know that's illegal?'

'Well,' said the captain, unabashed, 'you know us – we cheat!'

A First Division player not noted for his modesty was regaling his friends in the local pub. 'I came out of the ground after the match last Saturday and there were literally hundreds of fans outside waving autograph books at me!' Noticing the sceptical looks on the faces of his listeners, he added, 'It's quite true! If you don't believe me, ask Kenny Dalglish – he was standing right next to me!'

The rather unpopular secretary of a Fourth Division club was recently rushed to hospital with a suspected duodenal ulcer. The next day he received a get-well card from the club committee with the postscript: 'The decision to send you this card was carried by six votes to four, with two abstentions.'

Wife: 'Football, football, football! That's all you ever think about! If you said you were going to stay at home one Saturday afternoon to help with the house-work, I think I'd drop dead from the shock!'
Husband: 'It's no good trying to bribe me, dear.'

At a local derby between Arsenal and Spurs last season, a spectator suddenly found himself in the thick of dozens of flying bottles. 'There's nothing to worry about, lad,' said the elderly chap standing next to him. 'It's like the bombs during the war. You won't get hit unless the bottle's got your name on it.'

'That's just what I'm worried about,' said the fan. 'My name's Johnny Walker!'

Reporter: 'Tell me, Mr Harris, will your £100,000 win on the football pools make any difference to your way of life?'
Pools winner: 'None at all. I shall carry on exactly as before.'
Reporter: 'But what about all the begging letters?'
Pools winner: 'Oh, I'll keep sending them out as usual.'

In a crucial Cup semi-final a few years ago, the capacity crowd of 30,000 watched a rather diminutive striker get possession of the ball early in the second half. He was immediately tackled by three large defenders, and went down under a pile of thrashing arms and legs. Emerging dazed from the mêlée a few moments later, he looked round at the crowded stands and gasped, 'How did they all get back in their seats so quickly?'

A famous international footballer was asked to appear nude in the centrefold of a glossy new women's magazine. 'Our intention is to photograph you standing nude holding a ball,' said the features editor.

'I see,' said the footballer. 'What will I be doing with my other hand?'

The match was over and the team captain, who had muffed three easy goal shots, came over to the manager and said, 'You'll have to excuse me if I dash off, chief. I've got a plane to catch and I don't want to miss it.'

'Off you go, then,' said the manager. 'And better luck with the plane.'

The angry captain snarled at the referee. 'What would happen if I called you a blind bastard who couldn't make a correct decision to save his life?'

'It would be a red card for you.'

'And if I didn't say it but only thought it?'

'That's different. If you only thought it but didn't say it, I couldn't do a thing.'

'Well, we'll leave it like that, then, shall we?' smiled the captain.

'I hear you're from Wakefield. Does your town boast a football team?'

'We have a team, yes, but it's nothing to boast about.'

Striker: 'I've just had a good idea for strengthening the team.'

Manager: 'Good! When are you leaving?'

'We've got the best football team in the country – unbeaten and no goals scored against us!'

'How many games have you played?'

'The first one's next Saturday.'

A supporter arrived at the ground one Saturday to find the place completely empty. He went to the office and asked an official, 'What time does the match start?'

'There's no match today,' replied the official.

'But there must be!' argued the fan. 'It's Saturday.'

'I'm telling you there's no match today,' repeated the official.

'But there's always a match on Saturday afternoon,' said the fan, 'even if it's only a reserves game.'

'Watch my lips,' shouted the irate official. 'There is no M–A–T–F–C–H today!'

'Well, for your information,' the would-be spectator shouted back, 'there's no F in match.'

'That's what I've been trying to tell you!' yelled the official.

A man went off to a football match one Saturday afternoon, and while he was away his wife was visited by a 'friend' who just happened to be jogging past her house and was dressed in shorts and singlet. The wife was happily entertaining him on the sofa when suddenly they heard her husband coming through the front door. Quick as a flash, the visitor hid behind the large television set in the corner. The husband came in and said, 'It's started to pour with rain so I thought I'd come home and watch the second half on telly.' He switched on the television and settled down to watch the game. After about twenty minutes the wife's visitor started to get severe cramp so, casting caution to the winds, he calmly got up from behind the set and walked out of the room. The husband turned to his wife and said, 'That's funny – I didn't see the ref send him off.'

It is said that in Ireland, if it looks like rain before a match, they play the extra time first.

'Is your new striker fast?'
'Is he fast! He's so fast, the rest of the team have to run twice as fast just to keep up with him!'

Paddy: 'I couldn't get to the match last Saturday. What was the score?'
Mick: 'Nil–nil.'
Paddy: 'What was it at half-time?'

The manager and coach of an Irish team were discussing the players they had on their books and the manager asked, 'How many goals has O'Halloran scored this season?'

'Exactly double what he scored last season,' replied the coach. 'Eleven.'

'I just don't understand it,' an Irish footballer complained. 'One match I play very well, then the next match I'm terrible.'

'Well,' said his wife, 'why don't you just play every other match?'

'I don't care about results!' said an Irish team manager being interviewed on television. 'Just so long as our team wins!'

Two Irish team managers promised their players a pint of Guinness for every goal they scored during an important match. The final score was 119—98.

In the heat of the game, one of the players threw a vicious punch. The victim was all set to get stuck into him when the referee rushed up and held him back. 'Now then, O'Hara! You know you mustn't retaliate!'

'Come on, ref!' said O'Hara. 'He retaliated first!'

Three football codes prevail in Ireland: Rugby, which is defined as a thugs' game played by gentlemen; soccer – a gentleman's game played by thugs; and Gaelic football – a thugs' game played by thugs!

Two old men were holding up the queue outside the turnstyle before the game, while one of them hunted for his ticket. He looked in his coat pockets and his waistcoat pockets and his trouser pockets, all to no avail. 'Hang on a minute,' said the gateman. 'What's that in your mouth?' It was the missing ticket!

As they moved inside his mate said, 'Crikey, Cyril! You must be getting senile in your old age. Fancy having your ticket in your mouth and forgetting about it!'

'I'm not *that* stupid,' said old Cyril. 'I was chewing last week's date off it.'

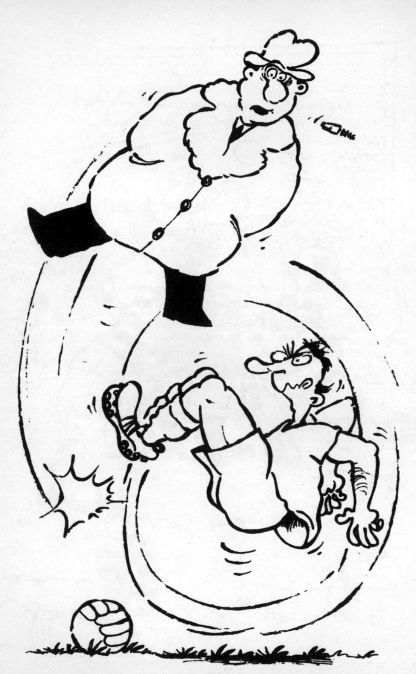

The manager of an Irish club was talking to a young player who had applied for a trial with the club. 'Do you kick with both feet?' asked the manager.

'Don't be silly!' said the trialist. 'If I did that, I wouldn't be able to stand up, would I?'

The rivalry between Celtic and Rangers in Scotland is well known. A Celtic fan looking for trouble went up to a perfect stranger in a pub in Sauchiehall Street and shouted in his ear: 'To hell with the Rangers!'

The stranger looked puzzled. 'I don't know what you're talking about, bud,' he said. 'I'm an American from Houston, Texas.'

The Celtic fan looked nonplussed for a moment but then, with a flash of inspiration, he yelled, 'To hell with the Texas Rangers, then!'

'My wife told me last week that she'd leave me if I didn't stop spending so much time at football matches.'

'What a shame!'

'Yes. I shall miss her.'

In church one Sunday the vicar opened his Bible to read the lesson. In a loud voice he proclaimed, 'Corinthians 7!'

A keen football fan who was dozing in the front row woke up with a start and shouted, 'Who were they playing?'

'We're starting up an amateur football team. Would you like to join?'

'I would, yes, but I'm afraid I don't know the first thing about football.'

'That's all right. We need a referee as well.'

After considerable effort and expense a First Division manager succeeded in obtaining the services of Miodrag Krivokapic and Mixu Paatelainen of Dundee, Dariusz Wdowczwk of Celtic, Detzi Kruszynski of Wimbledon, and Steve Ogrizovic of Coventry. 'Are these boys any good?' asked a colleague.

'I couldn't care less,' said the manager. 'I just want to get my own back on some of these smart-aleck TV sports commentators!'

The Football Association was considering a scheme for simplifying club badges and emblems so that they more closely reflected the clubs' names. A committee was set up to receive suggestions and, after a few weeks, the chairman called a meeting. 'Gentlemen,' he said, 'our request for new club badge designs has produced a very satisfactory response. Most of the suggestions are perfectly straightforward and logical – an ox for Oxford United, a sun for Sunderland, a heart for Heart of Midlothian, a windmill and a brick wall for Millwall. However, I'm afraid we must definitely draw the line at the proposed design received from Arsenal!'

'**I**s your goalkeeper getting any better?'
'Not really. Last Saturday he let in five goals in the first ten minutes. He was so fed up when he failed to stop the fifth that he put his head in his hands – and dropped it!'

As the defender ran in to tackle he took a full-blooded kick between the legs and fell unconscious to the ground. When he regained consciousness he was in hospital. He beckoned to the doctor and croaked, 'Is it bad?'

'I'm afraid so,' said the doctor.

'Are my playing days over?' asked the anxious footballer.

'Not necessarily,' answered the medic.

'So will I be able to play football for my club again?'

'Oh yes,' said the doctor, 'providing your club has a ladies team.'

'**J**ust a minute, ref!' yelled the goalkeeper. 'That wasn't a goal!'
'Oh, wasn't it?' shouted the referee. 'You just watch the "Sports Report" on television tonight!'

A big First Division team was very anxious to sign up a certain top-class player. However, nothing they offered would induce him to sign and in desperation they stooped to more underhand methods. The team manager sent his secretary – blonde, 5'2", 38—22—36 – to try to persuade the reluctant striker to sign up. To his surprise, he heard nothing from the girl for over a week. Then one morning she walked into his office and said, 'I've got good news and bad news for you, boss. The good news is – he's ready to sign. The bad news is – he's more than two stone down from his playing weight!'

A footballer was having a lot of trouble with his teeth so he went to see his dentist. 'What's the verdict?' he asked, after the dentist had carried out an examination.

'I forecast eight draws,' said the dentist.

It is said that the manager of a sports equipment company recently approached Nigel Spink, Aston Villa's goalkeeper and asked, 'For £20,000, would you endorse our football boots?'

'For £20,000,' said Nigel, 'I'd even *wear* your football boots!'

'Your team's rubbish! We beat you 9—2 last Saturday, even though we had a man short!'

'What do you mean "a man short"? You had ten players and the referee, didn't you?'

One of the top players in the 1990 England World Cup team was called as a character witness in a matrimonial case and, on being asked his profession, replied, 'I am the greatest footballer in the world!'

After the case was over he came in for a good deal of teasing from his team-mates. 'How could you stand up in court and say a thing like that?' they asked.

'Well,' he replied, 'you must remember I was under oath!'

A match took place recently in Oxford between a local amateur team and a side made up of university tutors and professors. Before the match the two captains faced each other while the referee flipped the coin to decide who would have choice of ends. The local team won the toss and, as the captain shook hands with his opposite number, he said sportingly,

'May the best team win!'

The university captain, a professor of English, replied, 'You mean, may the *better* team win!'

A football hooligan appeared in court charged with disorderly conduct and assault. The arresting officer, giving evidence, stated that the accused had thrown something into the canal. 'What exactly was it that he threw into the canal?' asked the magistrate.

'Stones, sir.'

'Well, that's hardly an offence is it?'

'It was in this case, sir,' said the police officer. 'Stones was the referee.'

Did you hear about the football captain in a minor league who was offered £1,000 to lose a game? It would have been against his principle to take the money but £1,000 against his principle looked pretty good so he took it.

A famous soccer international was talking to another guest at a party. 'I've been persuaded to write my autobiography,' he said, 'but I don't want it published until after I'm dead.'

'Really?' said the guest. 'I shall look forward to reading it.'

'You're all feet!' yelled the coach at the practice session. 'All bloody feet! How many times have I told you – use your brains, use your feet, but let the ball do the work!'

'Well, don't tell me,' shouted the unfortunate player. 'Tell the bloody ball!'

At a recent Irish League match between Newry and Larne, the visitors were awarded a penalty and the captain summoned his best player and said, 'I want you to take this one, Patrick. Just think hard as you kick – think which way the wind is blowing, and think which direction the keeper's going to jump.'

'Holy Mother!' said Patrick. 'Do you expect me to think and kick at the same time?'

'So you want to join us here at Leyton Orient as a goal-keeper, do you? What sort of salary were you expecting?'

'£500 a week.'

'And what experience have you had?'

'I've never played in goal before.'

'You've no goalkeeping experience and you want £500 a week!'

'Well, it's much harder when you don't know anything about it.'

Some years ago an important European match between England and Scotland was taking place in Milan. The referee was Hungarian. His command of English left a good deal to be desired and the players of both teams were taking the mickey out of him at every opportunity. Finally the Hungarian's patience ran out. 'You British!' he shouted. 'You think I know damn nothing about the game! Let me tell you – I know damn all!'

A big interdenominational football match was due to take place one Saturday between a team of Catholic priests and a team of rabbis. On the preceding Monday, disaster struck the Catholics. Their star player broke his leg! 'What are we going to do?' said Monsignor O'Reilly, the priests' manager.

'Well,' said Father O'Neal hesitantly, 'I know this is a little unethical, but Gary Lineker happens to be a good friend of mine. Maybe if we just referred to him as "Father Lineker", we could slip him into the team and . . .'

'Outrageous!' cried Monsignor O'Reilly. 'We'll do it!'

He was unable to attend the match personally on the Saturday, but at five o'clock Father O'Neal telephoned him with the result. 'Bad news, I'm afraid,' he said. 'The rabbis beat us 4–1.'

'What!' said Monsignor O'Reilly. 'Even with "Father Lineker" playing? Who scored for them?'

'Rabbi Gascoigne and Rabbi Beardsley,' said Father O'Neal.

GRAFFITI

Outside the County Ground at Swindon:

SWINDON TOWN ARE MAGIC!

And underneath:

WATCH THEM DISAPPEAR FROM THE SECOND DIVISION!

On the wall of a chapel in Dumbarton, Scotland:

JESUS SAVES!

And underneath:

DUMBARTON SHOULD SIGN HIM FOR GOAL!

On the toilet wall of a Second Division Club:
STOCKTON-ON-TEAS FOR THE CUP!

On a wall in the Republican area of Belfast:
BRITS OUT!
Under which someone had added:
EXCEPT CHARLTON, SATTERS, TOWNSEND, SHEEDY
AND ALDRIDGE.

A famous English footballer had just been trans-ferred for a record sum of money and was being interviewed on television. 'Do you realise,' said the interviewer, 'that the money you will receive as a result of this transfer, together with your income from endorsements, personal appearances, lecturing and so on will mean that you'll have earned more in one year than the Queen gets from the Civil List?'

'Well, I should hope so!' said the footballer. 'I play a damn sight better than she does.'

A man applied to Sheffield Wednesday FC for a job on the administrative staff. 'What we're really looking for here,' said the chairman, 'is what you might call a "chief worrier"! Someone to worry about things like falling attendances, finances, league promotion, violence on the terraces, and so on. For a chap like that we'd be prepared to pay £25,000 a year. Interested?'

'Certainly,' said the applicant. 'But – you'll pardon me for saying this, I hope – where on earth is Sheffield Wednesday going to find that sort of money for a job like this?'

'Ah!' said the chairman. 'That would be your first worry.'

The office-boy had taken the afternoon off to attend his uncle's funeral. His boss, a keen football fan, went the same afternoon to watch a match between Aberdeen and Celtic, and he saw the office-boy among the crowd. 'So this is your uncle's funeral, is it?' he said sarcastically.

'I shouldn't be at all surprised,' said the office-boy. 'He's the referee.'

A Ballymena United fan travelled to Bangor to see his team play the league leaders. He went into a pub for a few quick ones before the match but stayed rather too long and forgot about the game entirely. The match was long over when he left the pub and he caught the bus home and immediately fell asleep. He woke with a start some time later, and glancing out of the window, saw a sign which read BALLYMENA 30, BANGOR 20. 'Hurray!' he shouted. 'I knew we could beat the beggars!'

An amateur team in the West of Ireland played a match against a team from the local monastery. Just before the kick-off the visiting team, all of whom were monks, knelt down solemnly on the pitch, put their hands together and indulged in five minutes of silent prayer. The monastery then proceeded to trounce their hosts 9—0. After the match the home team captain said, 'Well, boys, we've been out-played before but this is the first time we've ever been out-prayed!'

A spectator at a match in the North of England kept up a constant barrage of insults and derogatory remarks directed against the referee. Finally the ref could stand it no longer. He marched over to the stand and, looking the noisy spectator squarely in the eye, shouted, 'Look here – I've been watching you for the last twenty minutes . . .'

'I thought so,' the spectator shouted back. 'I knew you couldn't have been watching the game!'

There was once a fanatical Spurs supporter who thought of nothing but football all day long. He talked about football, read about football, watched nothing but football on television and attended matches as often as he possibly could. At last his poor wife could stand it no longer. One night she said, 'I honestly believe you love Spurs more than you love me!'

'Blimey,' said the fan, 'I love Hartlepool United more than I love you!'

It was only the fourth week of the season and United's new goalkeeper had already let in twenty-seven goals. He was having a drink in a pub one night when a man approached him and said, 'I've been watching you play, son, and I think I might be able to help you.'

'Are you a trainer?' said the young goalkeeper hopefully.

'No,' said the stranger, 'I'm an optician.'

Did you hear what happened to old Andy McTavish last Saturday? He walked all the way to Wembley for the Cup Final to save on the train fare and then had to pay £20 to get in because he was too tired to climb over the wall!

There is only one recorded instance in soccer history of a goalkeeper being struck by lightning during a match. The goalkeeper was killed instantly and went straight to Heaven. He was greeted by an Archangel who offered to show him around. 'Would you like to see our football pitch?' asked the Archangel.

'Football pitch?' said the goalkeeper. 'Do you play football here?'

'Of course,' said the Archangel. 'We're playing Hell tomorrow in the Cup and we needed someone in goal. Why do you think we sent for you?'

Referee: 'Penalty!'
Home captain: 'Who for?'
Referee: 'Us!'

A well-known footballer who was just about to get hitched was holding forth in the local pub. 'It's generally thought,' he said, 'that when a player gets married, he loses his form, but that isn't going to happen to me. No – with Shirley by my side, I shall play better than ever!'

'I've been playing football professionally for ten years now. Of course, my father was dead set against my taking up the game at all. In fact he offered me £5,000 not to train.'

'Really? What did you do with the money?'

Irish football supporter: 'How much is it to come in?'
Ticket clerk: '£6. And that's standing room only.
Irish football supporter: 'Well, here's £3. I've only got one
                          leg.'

The manager of a Fourth Division club called his leading
goal-scorer into his office. 'You've played so well this
season,' he said, 'that the committee has decided to give you a
special bonus. We would like you to accept this cheque for
£500.'

'Thank you very much,' said the player. 'That's very kind of
you.'

'And,' continued the manager, 'if you play as well for the
rest of the season, the chairman will sign it for you.'

A man walked into the office of a large London firm and
said to the manager, 'I'm young Cartwright's grandfather
– he works in your mail room here. I just popped in to ask if
you could give him the afternoon off so I could take him to the
League Final at Wembley.'

'I'm afraid he's not here,' said the manager. 'We already gave
him the afternoon off to go to your funeral.'

A small boy stopped Derby County's Kevin Francis after a
League game and said, 'Could I have your autograph,
please?'

'But I gave you my autograph last week, didn't I?' said
Kevin.

'Yes, I know,' said the boy. 'But if I can get ten of yours, I
can swap them for one of Peter Shilton's.'

A week before the Cup Final at Wembley a few years ago there was an advertisement in *The Times* which read: 'Man offers marriage to woman supplying Cup Final ticket for next Saturday. Replies must enclose photograph of ticket.'

'You're looking worried.'
'Yes. My doctor's just told me I can't play football.'
'Oh! He's seen you play, has he?'

There was trouble on the terraces at The Hawthorns one Saturday afternoon. A huge West Bromwich Albion fan picked up a tiny spectator wearing the blue and white colours of Millwall, the visiting team. As he was about to hurl him to the ground, one of his mates yelled, 'Hey, Derek, don't waste him! Chuck him at the referee!'

A Manchester City fan came down to Wembley for the Cup Final. As he didn't have a ticket he asked a tout outside the gates how much the cheapest one cost. '£25,' said the tout.
'£25!' said the fan. 'Back in Manchester I could get a woman for that!'
'Maybe,' said the tout. 'But you wouldn't get an hour and a half with the Band of the Coldstream Guards in the interval!'

A woman was reading a newspaper one morning and said to her husband, 'Look at this, dear. There's an article here about a man who traded his wife for a season ticket to Arsenal. You wouldn't do a thing like that, would you?'
'Of course I wouldn't!' replied her husband. 'The season's almost over!'

There was once a football match between two small village teams. The visitors were surprised to see that the home team's goalkeeper was a horse. The horse played extremely well and it was mainly due to him that the home team won. After the match the visiting captain said to the home captain, 'How on earth did a horse ever learn to keep goal like that?'

'How does anyone learn?' answered the home captain. 'Practice, practice, practice!'

The shrill blast of the whistle and the pointing finger of the referee stopped the player in his tracks. The referee beckoned him over and produced notebook, pencil and yellow card. 'It's a yellow card for you,' said the referee, waving the card at the footballer.

'You know what you can do with your yellow card!' shouted the player.

'You're too late, mate,' replied the referee. 'There's three red cards there already!'

A visiting fan turned up at a Maidstone—Cardiff match last week and was told that seats were £6, £10 and £15, and programmes £1. 'OK,' he said cheerfully, 'I'll sit on a programme!'

'How did you enjoy your holiday in Israel?'
'Great!'
'Did you visit the Wailing Wall?'
'Yes – but I couldn't get near it for West Ham supporters!'

One of the Southern League's stadiums is several miles out of town, right next to a large farm. During a match one Saturday afternoon the ball was kicked clear out of the ground and landed in the farmyard in the middle of a group of chickens and a rooster. The rooster looked at the ball thoughtfully for a few moments and then said quietly, 'Ladies, I don't want to criticise, but I'd just like you all to take a look at the kind of work that's being turned out on other farms.'

A fellow had arranged to take his girlfriend to a local match but unfortunately they were delayed and didn't arrive until nearly half-time. 'What's the score?' the lad asked a bystander.

'Nil–nil,' was the reply.

'Oh, good!' his girlfriend gushed. 'We haven't missed anything!'

The boss called the office-boy into his private sanctum. 'How did your great-aunt's funeral go yesterday afternoon?' he asked.

'It went off all right, sir,' said the office-boy, puzzled.

'Good, good,' said the boss. 'Pity they've got to do it all over again.'

'Pardon, sir?' said the office-boy.

'Yes. I understand there's a replay on Saturday.'

'What's the best way to contact your long-lost relatives?' 'Win the football pools!'

A goalkeeper in the Second Division had the unfortunate habit of breaking wind when facing a penalty kick, a habit which was very off-putting for the kicker. On one occasion during an important cup match a penalty was awarded against his team. The striker placed the ball carefully, measured his run-up, cleaned the toe of his boot, and kicked. The ball went straight to the goalkeeper, who caught it cleanly without any bother.

'Sorry about that,' said the striker to his captain. 'It was his breaking wind that put me off.'

'But he didn't break wind this time,' replied the captain.

'No, I know,' said the striker. 'But I allowed for it.'

A bishop and a football manager both died on the same day and arrived at the Pearly Gates together. St Peter ignored the bishop but made a great fuss of the manager and welcomed him with open arms. The bishop was understandably puzzled over this and, approaching St Peter, he said, 'I don't want to be presumptuous, but I am a bishop and you haven't spoken a word to me. Yet that football manager is getting a rapturous welcome!'

'Well,' said St Peter, 'we get hundreds of bishops up here but this is the first football manager we've ever had!'

A famous footballer was killed in a car crash. Arriving in Heaven, he was greeted by the angel on duty at the gates. The angel took down the necessary particulars and then said, 'Is there anything you did on earth which would stop you from entering Heaven?'

'Well,' replied the footballer, 'I did once cheat in a very important football match.'

'Oh, dear!' cried the angel. 'Tell me what happened.'

'I was playing for Ireland against England and I scored a goal. I was offside at the time but the referee didn't notice and allowed the goal. As a result we won the match because that was the only goal scored.'

'Am I to understand that your action won the game for Ireland?' asked the angel.

'That is correct – and it's been worrying me for years.'

'Well, you can stop worrying. What you did was fine, so in you go!'

'Well!' said the player, pleasantly surprised. 'Thank you very much, Peter!'

'Oh, I'm not St Peter,' smiled the angel, 'I'm St Patrick!'

An unlucky footballer died and found himself outside the gates of Hell. 'Come in, come in!' said the devil on duty at the gate. 'We've been expecting you. You're Bill Rowlands, the famous footballer, aren't you?'

'That's right,' said Rowlands. 'Tell me, do you have any football pitches down here?'

'Oh yes,' said the devil. 'Dozens of them!'

'Great!' said the footballer. 'Of course, I haven't got any kit. I suppose you'll be able to supply boots and shorts – and, of course, a ball?'

'Boots and shorts, yes,' said the devil with a smile, 'but I'm afraid there are no balls down here.'

'What!' cried the footballer in astonishment. 'Dozens of pitches and not a single ball?'

'That's right,' said the devil. 'That's the hell of it!'

Tommy Docherty, the legendary manager, died and went straight up to Heaven. God said, 'Who are you?' as Docherty strode up to the Celestrial Throne.

'I'm Tommy Docherty,' he said. 'And that's my chair you're sitting in!'

There was once a big football match between Heaven and Hell for the Celestial Cup. An angel was talking to a devil on the night before the match and remarked, 'It should be a walkover for us, you know. We've got all the good footballers up here.'

'Yes, I know,' said the devil with a fiendish grin. 'But we've got all the referees down there!'

All through the match a well-dressed man in the crowd kept up a constant barrage of criticism directed at the referee. He questioned every decision and was scathing in his opinion of the referee's abilities and competence. When the game was over the referee went over to the heckler and asked him if he had a business card.

'Certainly,' said the man, somewhat surprised, and handed over a card on which was printed HENRY ADAMS, SOLICITOR.

'Thanks,' said the referee. 'I'll be in to see you on Monday morning.'

'All right,' said the solicitor. 'Legal problem, is it?'

'Oh, no, nothing like that,' said the referee. 'I'm just coming round to tell you how to run *your* business!'

A man holding a football leaned over his garden gate and shouted to two boys standing on the other side of the street, 'Is this your ball?'

'Did it do any damage, mister?' asked one of the lads.

'No, it didn't.'

'Then it's ours,' said the boy.

One boy asked another, 'Did I bring you back that football I borrowed last week?'

'No, you didn't,' said his pal.

'Damn!' said the first lad. 'I wanted to borrow it again!'

Two keen fans at a local derby were so engrossed in the match that, although they were both starving, they didn't want to take time out to go across to the refreshment stand. They noticed a young lad nearby and said, 'Here, kid, here's £1.50 – nip over there and get us a couple of hot-dogs, and one for yourself.'

A few minutes later the kid returned, chewing on a hot-dog, and handed them £1. 'Here's your change,' he said. 'They only had one hot-dog left.'

A small boy got lost at a football match. He went up to a policeman and said, 'I've lost my dad!'

The policeman said, 'What's he like?'

To which the little boy replied, 'Beer and women!'

At a school football match the goalkeeper collided with the goalpost and fell to the ground. Several boys gathered around him but, as his recovery appeared to be taking some time, the sportsmaster ran over to the group. 'What's the matter?' he asked.

'We're trying to give him the kiss of life, sir,' said one of the boys, 'but he keeps getting up and walking away!'

Two boys were playing football in the back garden with a
new football.

'Where did you get that ball?' asked their mother.

'We found it.'

'Are you sure it was lost?'

'Oh, yes. We saw them looking for it.'

At a World Cup game between England and West
Germany, the referee was a Brazilian who spoke very
little English. He had occasion to warn one of the England
players for tripping. When this happened a second time the
Brazilian referee said angrily, 'You trip again! Now is no more
tripping or is yellow card for you!' Ten minutes later the
English player committed yet another blatant foul.

The referee rushed up in a rage and, as he approached, the
English player said, 'Oh bugger off!'

The referee said, 'All right! As you have apologise, no card
this time. But next time – off!'

A shipwrecked sailor found himself on a remote island in
the Pacific. The only other inhabitant appeared to be a
very beautiful native girl. On the first day she fed him with
delicious native foods. On the second day she gave him lovely
cooling drinks. On the third day, to the sailor's surprise, she
produced a carton of cigarettes. By this time the sailor was
beginning to enjoy life on the island. On the fourth day the
girl smiled at him seductively and asked, 'Would you like to
play a game?'

'Blimey!' said the sailor. 'Don't tell me you've got a football
pitch on the island as well!'

There was once a famous football star who rather fancied himself as God's gift to the ladies. He fell in love with a local girl and approached her father to ask for permission to marry her.

'My daughter marry a football player?' shouted the father. 'Over my dead body!'

'But, sir, you haven't even seen me play!' protested the star.

'Well, all right, then – I'll come to the match on Saturday.'

After the match the father came into the dressing rooms and shook the footballer warmly by the hand. 'Of course you can marry my daughter, my boy! You're no more a football player than I am!'

After the season was over a couple of the players used their savings to go on safari in Africa. The highlight of their trip was seeing a lion in his natural habitat after making a kill. Suddenly the lion began to walk purposefully towards them. One of the players immediately began to put on a pair of jogging shoes. His friend said, 'You're wasting your time! You'll never outrun that lion!'

'Maybe not,' said his friend, 'but if I can outrun you, I'll be laughing!'

Milligan went to see his home team play one Saturday afternoon and lost £20 betting on the home side. After dinner that evening he went to the pub where the match was being shown on television. 'I'll bet any man here £20 the home side wins!' he roared.

Several of the regulars took him up on the bet with the result that he lost a small fortune. When he got home he told his wife what had happened.

'You great idiot!' she shouted. 'Why did you bet on a home

win when you'd seen the home team get beat this afternoon?'

'Well,' said Milligan, 'I didn't think they'd make the same mistakes twice!'

A woman wanted to go to a football match with her husband, who was a keen follower of the game, so he agreed to take her to the next available match. It took her some time to decide what to wear and they arrived just in time for the kick-off. Her husband was soon shouting and yelling with the rest of the crowd, but it was obvious she hadn't a clue what it was all about.

'Look, darling,' her husband explained slowly, 'the object of the game is to get the ball into one or other of the nets at each end of the field.'

'Wouldn't it be easier,' said his wife, 'if they didn't get in each other's way so much?'

'Who's this Bill Baker everyone's talking about?'

'You mean to say you don't know? He's the bloke that saved United from relegation last Saturday.'

'What position does he play?'

'Position? He doesn't play – he was the referee.'

It was a needle match between Celtic and Rangers at Glasgow's Ibrox Park. A mild little man was accosted by a huge and aggressive supporter in full regalia. 'Are ye a Celtic fan or a Rangers fan?' he growled menacingly.

'Neither, really,' said the little man nervously. 'I just like watching football.'

'Och,' snarled the Scot, 'a bloody atheist, eh?'

Joe was admiring a silver cup in a display cabinet. It was inscribed TO THE FOOTBALLER OF THE YEAR. 'Hey, Mickey,' he said, 'I didn't know you were interested in football.'

'I'm not,' said Mickey.

'But you've got a silver cup inscribed to the footballer of the year in your cabinet.'

'Oh, I got that for running.'

'Running?' said Joe. 'How the hell did you get a football cup for running?'

'Simple,' said Mickey. 'When no one was looking, I grabbed it and ran.'

A certain Fourth Division club was right at the bottom of the ladder so the coach instituted a course of retraining for the coming season. As many of the team members seemed to be ignorant of the basics of the game, he decided to start at the beginning. He picked up a ball and said, 'Now, gentlemen, the object I'm holding is called a football. Now the object of the game is . . .'

From the back came an agitated voice: 'Hang on a minute, coach! Not so fast!'

A football widow was complaining to her husband that his passion for the game was ruining their marriage. 'You never take me out,' she wailed. 'You never buy me presents. You're never at home if there's a match on anywhere. You never even remember our anniversary. Why I'll bet you've even forgotten the date of our wedding!'

'Of course I haven't!' scoffed her husband. 'It was the day Sweden beat Germany in the UEFA Under-Eighteen Championship at Lomma!'

Another Elephants United match that has gone down in the annals of soccer history is the one they played against a team composed entirely of ants – Ants Athletic. Shortly before half-time, one of the Elephant defenders stepped on the Ants' striker and squashed him flat. 'Sorry about that, ref,' he said apologetically, 'I only meant to trip him.'

A player was taken to hospital with a dislocated knee, incurred during a match, and his agonised roarings were heard all over casualty as the doctor tried to put the joint back into place. Said the doctor, 'For a supposedly hardened League player, you're making a hell of a lot of fuss. There's a woman next door who's having a baby and she isn't making half the fuss you're making!'

'Maybe so,' said the injured player. 'But in her case, nobody's trying to push anything back in!'

'I played in a match last week with Maradona!'
'You didn't!'
'Yes, I did. He said to me, "If you're a footballer I'm Maradona!"'

A talent scout for a First Division team was touring Ireland. He attended a local match between two small town teams and was amazed by the skill of one of the players. He approached the player after the match and offered him a place in the First Division team, with a very attractive salary. 'We'd like to have you,' he said, 'and if there's anything you want, or any special requests, you only have to ask.'

'Well,' said the local man, 'I would like to join your team but there is one condition.'

'What is it?'

'I'd like to have Saturday afternoons off to play for my old team.'

No collection of football anecdotes would be complete without mention of the legendary Elephants United team. On one occasion the Elephants (playing at their home ground Pachyderm Park, in their usual colours – grey trunks) were matched against a team of Insects. By half-time in this somewhat one-sided match, the Elephants were leading by 149 goals to nil. At the start of the second half, however, the Insects sent in a new forward, a centipede. Immediately the game changed and the Insects took command of the match. The centipede scored again and again, and proved to be completely unstoppable. The final score was 703 goals to 150 in the Insects' favour.

After the match the Elephant captain said to his opposite number, a water-beetle, 'That centipede of yours was great! I can't understand why you didn't use him from the start.'

'We would have done, believe me,' said the Insect captain, 'but it takes him forty-five minutes to get his boots on.'

'Shoot, Gazza, shoot!' yelled a fan at a crucial moment in England's World Cup match against Italy.

'Shoot Gazza!' said his disgruntled neighbour. 'I wish they'd shoot the whole ruddy lot of them!'

A group of supporters of the local football team assembled outside the gates just before kick-off and discovered that one member was missing. 'Oh, yes, I remember,' said one of them. 'Harry said something about getting married this afternoon at two-thirty.'

'You must be joking!' said his neighbour. 'That means he won't get here until half-time!'

The home captain was talking to the visiting referee. 'Now we don't expect any favouritism,' he said. 'However, I'd like to point out that our ground is next to a hospital and there's a canal over on the far side – and we haven't lost a home match all season.'

A bald-headed goalkeeper jumped frantically at an incoming ball and headed it into his own goal. 'Oi, mate!' shouted a voice from the crowd. 'You forgot to chalk yer cue!'

A Fourth Division goalkeeper missed a simple kick at goal and as he picked up the ball from the back of the net, a spectator shouted, 'Call yourself a goalkeeper? I could have caught that shot in me mouth!'

'So could I,' the goalkeeper yelled back, 'if my mouth was as big as yours!'

A Fourth Division team was about to play the First Division leaders in a Cup match, and the manager was giving them a last-minute pep-talk. 'All right, lads,' he said. 'Go out there and slay them! You'll be the giant-killers of the decade. And then I'll get enough money to replace the lot of you!'

One Saturday morning a man was standing at the bar staring thoughtfully into his pint of beer. A friend approached and asked, 'What's bothering you, Joe? You're really deep in thought.'

'Well,' said Joe, 'this morning my wife ran away with my best friend.'

'Joe!' said his friend sympathetically. 'That's terrible!'

'It certainly is,' agreed Joe. 'It means we're short of a goalkeeper for the match this afternoon.'

England was playing Ireland and the ground was packed. There wasn't an empty seat – except for the one next to Mike Murphy. Mike's friend, Pat, tapped him on the shoulder and said, 'How come you have an empty seat beside you?'

'Oh, that was for the wife,' said Mike.

'Didn't she want to come to the match?'

'It's not that. You see, she died three days ago.'

'Oh, I am sorry,' said Pat. 'Couldn't one of your friends have come instead so as not to waste the seat?'

'Not really,' answered Mike. 'They all wanted to go to the funeral.'

Little Jimmy came home from school one day and let himself into the house. Everything was quiet and he tiptoed to his room. As he passed his mother's door he saw her sitting at the dressing table, hugging herself and moaning, 'I want a man! I want a man!' Jimmy was puzzled but went off to his room without disturbing her. Next day the same thing happened. Again he saw his mother hugging herself and moaning, 'I want a man! I want a man!' The third day, when Jimmy came past his mother's room, she was lying on the bed with a strange man. Quick as a flash, Jimmy ran to his room, sat down in front of the mirror and started chanting, 'I want a pair of football boots! I want a pair of football boots!'

A forward had a reputation for very hard play and following a match one day he returned to the dressing room with a hell of a leg on him: lacerations down the shin-bone, dislocated knee cap, bruising to the thigh and grazes everywhere. The only trouble was he didn't know who the leg belonged to.

The championship team had been playing away, and after the match the bus they were travelling home in was involved in a serious accident. The driver, the manager, and all the players were killed instantly. The only survivor was the team mascot – a chimpanzee. Soon after the disaster, investigators came out to determine the cause of the accident. They interviewed the chimp, who gave all his answers in sign language.

'Just before the crash, what was the driver doing?'

The chimp made signs to indicate drinking and smoking.

'And what was the manager doing?'

More signs of drinking and smoking.

'And the rest of the team?'

Actions of drinking and smoking and general carrying-on.

'This is terrible!' said one of the investigators. 'They must have been having some kind of party on the bus!' Then, turning to the chimp, he asked, 'What were *you* doing just before the crash?'

Whereupon the chimp went through the motions of driving a bus.

Boss: 'You told me you were going to see your dentist yesterday, but I saw you at White Hart Lane with a friend.

Employee: 'That's right, sir – that was my dentist.'

The goalkeeper wasn't looking at all happy and a friend said, 'I hear you didn't do so well in goal this afternoon.'

'Listen,' said the goalkeeper. 'If I hadn't been there, we'd have lost 25–nil!'

'Oh? What was the final score then?'

'24–nil!'

As the funeral procession passed along the street a passer-by noticed a pair of football boots on the coffin which was being carried by four young men. He nudged the man standing next to him and, pointing to the boots, said, 'Well-known footballer, was he?'

'Oh, no,' came the reply. 'Those belong to one of the bearers. He kicks off at two-thirty.'

On the day Aldershot lost 10–1 at Southend in the Leyland Daf Cup, Len Walker, the Aldershot manager, was seen walking through the town with a video recorder under his arm. 'What's the recorder for, Len?' asked a passing fan.

'I got it for the team,' said the beleaguered manager.

'Reckon you got a damned good bargain then,' said the disgruntled supporter.

It is recorded with great authority that, in the days when players received a maximum wage and also different rates for the winter and summer periods, the legendary Tom Finney left the manager's office, having negotiated the coming season. 'What did you get, Tom?' asked his team-mate, waiting his turn.

'£12 a week, winter and summer,' replied the Peerless Plumber.

The team-mate took his place in the manager's office. 'Now then, lad,' said the manager, 'you've not done bad, so I'm giving you a new contract. You'll get £12 a week in the winter and £8 in the summer.'

'But, gaffer,' protested the player, 'Finney's getting £12 a week all year!'

'Yes, son,' frowned the manager, 'but he's a better player than you.'

'Not in the summer, he's not!' was the explosive retort.

A team manager came home unexpectedly one evening when a game he was due to watch was called off. He found the house in darkness, slipped in quietly, mounted the stairs and switched on the bedroom light to discover his assistant in bed with his wife. 'Tommy!' he said sadly. 'I *have* to. But you?'

Two small boys wearing T-shirts were spotted on the beach at Southend. One shirt carried the legend LABOUR WINS SOUTHEND EAST! The other boy's T-shirt read: SOUTHEND UNITED WIN EUROPEAN CUP! The two lads went into the sea for a swim and swam quite a way out. Suddenly the onlookers saw to their horror the dreaded triangular fin of a shark accelerating towards the boys through the water. The watchers could only stand there as first one boy and then the other disappeared under the waves. But after a couple of minutes one of the boys reappeared and made his way, ashore.

He was helped out of the water by the former MP for Southend, Teddy Taylor. As Teddy lifted the boy up he noticed that the survivor wore the shirt bearing the legend: SOUTHEND UNITED WIN EUROPEAN CUP! 'Are you all right?' he said solicitously. 'How was it that the shark ate your friend but let you go?'

The boy pointed to his T-shirt. 'No problem, Mr Taylor,' he said. 'Not even a shark could swallow this!'

It is the custom for vociferous football supporters to chant the name of their team, letter by letter. Thus Tottenham Hotspur fans will shout, 'Give us an S, give us a P, give us a U . . .' and so on. Brian Naysmith, Fulham's chief executive, suggests that the most hated German football fan is the one who stands on the terraces of Borussia Mönchengladbach and shouts, 'Give us a B, give us an O, give us an R . . .!'

There's a little grocer's shop just around the corner from London's Connaught Rooms, and one morning a man walked in and bought up all the rotten eggs, old tomatoes and cabbages on the shelves. The assistant grinned. 'I bet you're going to that talk Brian Clough's giving tonight at the Connaught Rooms, about the England World Cup team!'

'No,' said the stranger. 'I *am* Brian Clough!'

There was once a manager of a small and unsuccessful Fourth Division club who had a rather inflated notion of his own prowess and leadership. He attended a convention of club managers at the Savoy Hotel and fell into conversation with a well-known sports commentator. Looking round at the assembled team bosses, he remarked, 'How many great club managers do you think there are in this room?'

'One less than you think!' replied the commentator.

A team manager was once having a drink in a pub when a horse walked in and ordered a pint of lager. They fell into conversation and the horse revealed that he was himself a keen player. 'Is there a chance of getting a trial for your club?' he asked.

'What position do you play?' asked the manager.

'Goalkeeper,' replied the horse.

The manager, who had a nose for talent, invited the horse to turn out for the team on the following Saturday. The horse accepted. For four consecutive Saturdays the horse played for the team and not once did the ball pass him. He was superb! After the fourth game the manager said, 'You're playing brilliantly in goal, but as we're not scoring any ourselves, I'm thinking of pushing you up the field and making you a striker.'

'But that would mean I'd have to run!' protested the horse.

'Of course you'd have to run!' said the manager.

'But I can't run!' said the horse. 'If I could run, I'd be at Ascot instead of here playing this bloody stupid game!'

During the 1920s there was a certain Lord Kinnaird who, in his youth had been a keen footballer. He used to tell the story of a match in which he took part: an opposing forward made a very tricky run and Kinnaird went to tackle him, feeling quite confident of getting the ball away from him. But as he approached, the opposing forward said, 'Let me score! I want to get my name in the papers!'

'He did score, too,' said Lord Kinnaird, 'for I was so tickled that I couldn't do a thing! He easily dribbled round me, and shot straight into the net!'

Two rival football managers, Connors and Hargreaves, were continually trying to outdo each other. Whatever improvements Connors introduced into his club, Hargreaves had to go one better. When Connors had floodlights installed, Hargreaves had a new stand built. When Connors ordered new luxury coaches to transport the team to away matches, Hargreaves installed closed-circuit television. Then Connors bought a vintage Bentley worth £30,000. Shortly afterwards, Hargreaves acquired a white Rolls-Royce with a built-in bar. Connors countered by having a car-phone installed in his Bentley and immediately Hargreaves did the same. To show that he was keeping up with his rival, Hargreaves made a call from his Rolls-Royce to Connors' Bentley. Connors' chauffeur answered the call. 'I'd like to speak to Mr Connors, please,' said Hargreaves smugly.

'I'm sorry, sir,' said the chauffeur. 'Mr Connors is taking a call on the other line.'

There was once a famous football coach who was notorious for his shortsightedness and for his bad temper. He was conducting a training session on one occasion and noticed that the players were somewhat listless and inattentive. Losing his temper, he shouted, '*You* at the back of the room! What should the full-back do if he's playing on the right and there's a break through on the opposite side of the field?'

'I don't know,' said the chap at the back.

'Well, then, can you tell me the rules governing the defence position when a penalty is being taken?'

'I don't know.'

'I taught you that only yesterday!' bellowed the coach. 'Didn't you hear what I said?'

'I wasn't here,' said the man.

'Where were you then?'

'I was having a few drinks with some friends.'

The coach turned purple. 'You have the audacity to tell me that! How do you expect to improve?'

'I don't, coach. I'm an electrician and I just came in here to fix the lights.'

A disgraceful brawl took place at a recent Southern League match and on the following Wednesday evening a tribunal met to determine the cause of the incident. They called in the captain of the home team and said, 'Will you tell the tribunal in your own words how the fight started.'

'I didn't see any fight,' said the captain.

'You didn't? Well then tell us what you did see.'

'Well,' said the captain, 'Parker elbowed Thomas in the stomach, and as he went down, he put his hand in the mud and Bannerman stood on it. Then Parker's mate, Gibson, punched Bannerman in the mouth and knocked out a couple of teeth. Thomas got up and flattened Parker, and I could see the whole thing was probably going to turn into a fight, so I left the pitch.'

The village football team found itself short of a goalkeeper at an important match one Saturday afternoon. Rather than play a man short, the captain asked a young man who was standing on the touchline if he would go into goal.

'Oh, I don't know anything about the game,' said the man.

'That's all right,' said the captain. 'All you have to do is make sure the ball doesn't go between the posts.'

Reluctantly, the young man agreed to play, and by half-time he had let in eight goals without making any attempt to stop them.

'You might at least try to stop the ball!' said the captain. 'I did explain what you had to do!'

'Yes, I know what you said,' replied the young man 'but I don't see why I should throw myself all over the place to try and stop the ball when there's a perfectly good net there for that very purpose!'

For the third time in the first ten minutes of the match the referee awarded a penalty against the home team. An angry supporter shouted, 'Oi, ref, are you blind or what?'

The referee strode over to the touchline and demanded, 'What was that you said?'

'Blimey' the fan shouted back, 'Are you deaf as well?'

'Was there a big crowd at the match on Saturday?'

'Big crowd? There were so few of us, the players gave us a round of applause when we walked in!'

I went to Highbury last Saturday and I've never seen so many people trying to get into a match! I said to the fellow next to me, 'Do you think we'll get in?'

He said, 'I hope so! I'm the referee!'

A former footballer who had become rather corpulent was asked to turn out for a charity match but he refused. 'I'm so disappointed!' said the organiser. 'Won't you change your mind?'

'No, son, I won't,' said the ex-footballer. 'I tried it a few years ago. As soon as the ball came towards me, my brain rapped out all the old commands – run towards the ball at speed, trap it, beat the defender, kick for goal . . . !'

'So it's all still there, then!' said the organiser.

'No, it isn't. You see, when my brain rapped out the orders, my body said, "Who me?"'

A new amateur team had just been formed in a northern mining town. Just before their first match the team captain addressed the lads. 'Now remember, boys,' he said, 'if you don't have possession, go for their shins or their ankles. Trip 'em up, and when they're down, make sure they stay down. Now then – who's got the ball?

'Never mind the ball,' said a voice from the back. 'Let's get on with the bloody game!'

A television programme called 'Great Sportsmen of the Past' was being prepared recently and a researcher was sent to interview a former footballer now in his nineties. The fellow had done his preliminary research and knew he was in the presence of one of the all-time greats of football. His skill on the field had been unequalled, his sportsmanship renowned. After a very interesting interview the researcher said, 'One last question, sir. In your long and outstanding career as a footballer, is there anything you would change if you had to do it all over again?'

The old footballer pondered for a moment and then answered, 'Yes. I'd probably let my moustache grow longer.'

A centipede applied for a trial with a football team and was being interviewed by the coach. 'What position do you play?' asked the coach.

'I'm a striker,' said the centipede.

'Interesting,' said the coach. 'Which is your kicking foot?'

'I can kick with my left or my right,' said the centipede, 'but my best foot is my right, my right, my right, my right, my right, my right . . .'

'My brother's got dozens of trophies and medals for football.'

'Does he play for England?'

'He doesn't play at all. He owns a pawnshop.'

The local beauty queen was the guest of honour at a celebration given by a football team which had just won the Southern League championship. In her speech she pointed out that the life of a beauty queen was very similar to that of a footballer. 'In fact,' she said, 'I've probably worked out more defences against passes than any of you here tonight!'

'I hear your team took your 21—0 defeat last Saturday very badly.'

'Yes, they did.'

'Sad about the goalkeeper. Could some of the players not have stopped him hanging himself from the goalposts?'

'Stopped him! Who the hell do you think helped him tie the rope to the crossbar?'

Two men were sitting in a pub watching 'Match of the Day' on television. It was a First Division game and one of the men remarked, 'You know, the manager of the home team was trying to get me for months.'

'Was he?' said his friend. 'Who were you playing with at the time?'

'His wife!'

'Do you know,' asked the vicar, 'what happens to little boys who play football every Sunday afternoon instead of coming to Bible class?'

'Yes,' replied little Sammy. 'They grow up to play in the First Division, become international stars, appear on television, and get very, very rich!'

The Cup Final was being shown on television and a viewer was yelling and shouting as loudly as the fans at the ground. 'I can't understand what all the fuss is about,' said his wife as she handed him a cup of tea. 'I thought they decided who the champions were last year!'

'I hear your football club is looking for a treasurer.'
'That's right.'
'But didn't you take on a new treasurer last month?'
'Yes – that's the one we're looking for!'

The girls in the factory had accepted a challenge football match with the men. They insisted on having a training session first and the men agreed that they would leave the ground and let the girls practise unobserved. On the evening in question, the men finished their training session and, as arranged left the field. The girls went out onto the field, selected two teams and were just about to start when they realised they hadn't got a ball. One of the girls was sent to the pavilion to get one but returned empty-handed. 'All the men have gone home,' she wailed, 'and taken their balls with them!'

A man had a son in the local team and never missed a match. However, one Saturday afternoon the team had an away match and he was unable to attend the game. He asked his son to telephone the result as soon as the game was over. When the call came through his wife picked up the telephone and after listening for a few moments, reported, 'It's Tom – he says he's had his nose broken, some teeth knocked out, and he's lost an ear!'

'Yes, yes,' said the father impatiently. 'But who won?'

The coach was tearing a strip off his star centre-half. 'Your game's gone all to hell,' he said, 'and I know the reason why. You're meant to be in training. See that you stay away from women until the end of the season! I don't want to hear about you taking a girl out again. Is that clear?'

'OK, OK,' said the player. 'No more dates until the end of the season.'

However, the next day the coach was walking down the street when who should he bump into but the same player with a voluptuous blonde on his arm.

'Now look,' said the player. 'Don't get excited! This lady is my wife.'

'*Your* wife!' roared the coach. 'Why, you bastard – that's *my* wife!'

At the end of every football season, every keen football fan has to go through the same ritual:

1. Relearn the names of all his children.
2. Replace the springs in the sofa.
3. Sign up his wife for a course in remedial sex.

There was a report last week that a British underwear company brought out a new brassiere to coincide with the 1990 World Cup. They called it 'Scotland' – it had plenty of support but no cups.

Overheard in the boardroom: 'He's definitely an honest referee. When he's bought, he stays bought.'

One of the senior members of the football club was attending a club dinner. About halfway through he telephoned his wife. 'You know, my dear,' he said, 'there's something very unexpected here. I thought it would be just drinking and speeches, but there are naked girls dancing on the tables, and they're going under the tables with the men. What do you think I should do?'

'If you think you can do anything,' said the wife, 'come home immediately!'

A chap somewhat the worse for liquor staggered up to the turnstiles at a Wigan home match last Saturday. 'I'm not selling you a ticket,' said the attendant. 'You're drunk!'

'Of course I'm drunk!' said the man. 'You don't think I'd come to a Wigan match sober, do you?'

'I hear you've got a new job?'
'That's right. It's one of the easiest jobs I've ever had.'
'What do you do?'
'I keep score for Stockport County.'

At a recent match between Everton and Liverpool a huge supporter wearing the home team's blue and white colours suddenly turned to a meek little man in Liverpool's reds and punched him on the nose.

'Was that meant as a joke?' said the little man.

'No, it wasn't!' bellowed the six-footer.

'That's all right, then,' said the little Liverpool supporter. 'I don't like jokes like that.'

Reporter: 'Congratulations on your big pools win! £200,000! That's quite a tidy sum. What are you going to do with it all?'

Pools winner: 'I'm going to take a cruise round the world, staying in all the best hotels – that'll cost me about £50,000. Then I'll spend £50,000 on the horses and cards, £30,000 on women, and £20,000 on boozing it up.'

Reporter: 'And what about the remaining £50,000?'

Pools winner: 'Oh, I'll probably just blow that!'

A businessman came home one evening in a thoroughly bad mood. His wife asked him, 'What's got into you?'

'One of the juniors asked for the afternoon off to go to his grandmother's funeral. I thought it was the old trick to get to the football game, so I followed him.'

'Was it a good game?' asked the wife.

'Game be damned! It *was* his grandmother's funeral!'

Mother: 'Well, how did you like your visit to the British Museum with Daddy?'

Billy: 'Great! Our team won 5—3!'

It had been a bad day for the club's leading striker. Six times goals had been set up for him, and six times he had missed. As he entered the dressing room, he asked, 'Has anyone got 10p? I want to telephone a friend.'

'Here's 20p,' said the captain. 'Telephone all your friends!'

A footballer broke his leg in a home match one Saturday afternoon and had to go to hospital. A few days later one of the other players visited him. The injured footballer was by no means the team's best player, and was rather worried about losing his place on the team.

'Oh, you don't want to worry about that,' said his fellow-player. 'Why, everyone's been talking about you. Only yesterday, the captain said, "Whatever happened to old what's-his-name?"'

A couple of fans turned up recently at Doncaster's Belle Vue ground, handed over £20 and said, 'Two, please.'

'Right,' said the ticket clerk. 'What would you like – strikers, wing-halves, full-backs . . . ?'

Punter: '£50 on Liverpool to beat Dundee.'
Bookie: 'Sorry – we don't take bets on friendlies.'
Punter: 'Don't be daft! Liverpool don't play friendlies!'

'What happens exactly at a football match?'

'Well, two teams of eleven players each go on to a large field and they try to kick a ball into a net while another person, called a referee, watches them.'

'What happens when the referee isn't watching them?'

'Well, then they kick each other.'

A famous football coach was finishing his pep-talk to the team just before an important match. 'Remember, men,' he said, 'football builds leadership, initiative and individuality! Now get out on to that field and do exactly as I've told you!'

Woody had played like a hairy goat all afternoon. When the team came off the ground after the final whistle, he said sheepishly to the coach, 'Sorry about that. I'm not playing my usual game today.'

'What game is that then?' said the coach. 'Croquet?'

An Irish team was visiting Spain on an international tour. Their first evening was free and one player went to another hotel to have a drink. He was sitting at the bar when an attractive Spanish girl came up and sat on the stool next to him. 'Hello,' said the player. 'Do you speak English?'

'Jos a leetle bit,' she smiled.

'How much?' asked the footballer.

'£25,' said the girl seductively.

'What happened at the game today?' asked Billy.

'That bloody referee was playing for the other side,' answered Andy. 'Three of our fellows got fouled. Smith got an elbow in the eye, Martin got a kick on the knee, and Hoffman got a knee in the crutch! And all the referee could say was that he wasn't in the right position to see the fouls!'

'Wasn't he in position to see anything?'

'Only when Smith punched him on the nose – he was perfectly positioned for that!'

There was a report in the paper last week about a young man who won £250,000 on the football pools. Apparently he had told his mother and father that he was generously going to give them £50 each out of his winnings. The old couple were so upset that the father confessed that they were not the young man's real parents. 'What!' he yelled. 'Are you telling me that I'm a bastard?'

'You are that,' said his father. 'And a damn mean one at that!'

'That new centre-forward is a steady player, isn't he.'

'Steady? If he was any steadier, he'd be motionless.'

Tall spectator at football match: 'What a crowd! Why, there must be 30,000 people watching the game this afternoon!'

Small spectator standing behind him: 'Well, let's just say 29,999!'

A policeman on duty at a football ground saw a man with a gorilla walking towards him. He approached the man and said, 'Didn't I speak to you yesterday about that gorilla?'

'That's right, officer,' said the man. 'I found him wandering in the streets and I asked you what I should do with him.'

'And I told you to take it to the zoo.'

'Yes, you did, and I took him to the zoo and he enjoyed it so much, today I thought I'd bring him to a football match!'

A soccer fan has been defined as someone sitting several hundred feet from the ball who can see it better than the referee standing right next to it.

A team manager was talking to a young man who wanted to become a professional footballer. 'You must understand,' he said, 'that if you want to be a really good footballer, the best thing is to give up smoking, drinking and girls.'

'I see,' said the young man thoughtfully. 'Tell me, what's the next best thing?'

Two fans were standing together in the pouring rain, watching the slowest game they had seen all season.

'Tell me again about all the fun we're having,' said one. 'I keep forgetting.'

Did you hear about the Scotsman who sued a Scottish League club because he was injured while watching a match? He fell out of the tree.

First Irishman: 'There's a girl at work who's so stupid, she thinks a football coach has four wheels!'
Second Irishman: 'Would you believe that! How many wheels does it have?'

First wife: 'I find football very educational.'
Second wife: 'How is that?'
First wife: 'Every time my husband turns on the television to watch football, I go into another room and read a book.'

Did you hear about the amateur footballer who was caught accepting payments for matches? He lost his amateur standing so he turned professional and now he's broke.

First girl: 'I hear your Joe's joined United. What position does he play?'
Second girl: 'I'm not sure but I heard some of the other players say he was their main drawback.'

Coach: 'Do you know why you don't score more goals?'
Striker: 'I just can't think.'
Coach: 'That's right!'

A man lay in bed suffering from shock after checking his football coupon to find he had the only eight draws on the Treble Chance and had won £750,000. The doctor examined him and then came downstairs and said to his wife, 'I think he's all right now. He's over the worst of the shock.'

'Oh, good,' said the wife. 'Do you think it's safe to tell him I forgot to post his coupon?'

A fan took his girlfriend to a game for the first time. She couldn't understand what was going on at all and had no idea about the functions of each player. 'What's that man doing standing at the big net?' she asked.

'He's the goalkeeper,' said her boyfriend. 'He has to make sure that the ball doesn't go into the net.'

'And how much does he get for that?'

'Oh, I don't know – about £20,000 a year.'

'Good gracious,' said the young lady. 'Wouldn't it be cheaper to have it boarded up?'

The goalkeeper fancied himself as the star of the team and was very free with his advice to the captain. One Saturday afternoon, as the teams went on to the field he said to the captain. 'You know, you've picked two men this afternoon who should never be in the team at all.'

'Really?' said the captain. 'Who's the other one?'

The referee rushed over to where the player was writhing on the ground just outside the penalty area. 'Did you see who it was that hit you?' he asked.

'No,' groaned the player. 'But I got a note of his number.'

Two Greek immigrants were watching their very first football game. After a few minutes of mystified silence, one turned to the other and said, 'You know, this is all English to me!'

Did you read about that First Division footballer who retired last week with £750,000 in the bank? He claimed that it was due to hard work, perseverance, dedication to the game, and the fact that his uncle died last month and left him £745,000.

Striker: 'Sorry about missing that last goal, chief. I know it was an easy one, and believe me, I could kick myself.'

Coach: 'I shouldn't bother. You'd probably miss.'

'Aren't you going to the Bradford City match this Saturday?'

'Why the hell should I? They didn't come to see me when I was bad!'

After a disastrous game the coach got stuck into one of the worst offenders. 'Fosdyke, you're playing like an old woman! You should be ashamed of yourself! You're useless – a liability to the team!'

After the coach had left, one of Fosdyke's mates tried to console him. 'Don't take any notice of the coach,' he said comfortingly. 'He only repeats what he hears everyone else saying.'

A young Crystal Palace defender had been playing badly all season. Deciding it was time to pull his socks up, he went out one Saturday afternoon and gave it all he'd got. Proud of his efforts, he sought out the coach after the game and asked, 'Well, coach have you noticed any improvement in me since last week?'

The coach looked at him for a moment and then said, 'You've had a haircut!'

The road to Wembley stadium was crowded with fans making their way to the Cup Final. Suddenly a funeral procession passed by, and one fan reverently removed his cap.

'That was a nice gesture,' said his mate.

'It was the least I could do,' said the fan. 'She was a good wife to me for thirty years.'

An ex-player was holding forth in his local to a group of hangers-on. 'When I was playing professionally,' he said, 'I helped Manchester United beat Leeds for three seasons running.'

'Really?' said one listener. 'Which side were you playing for?'

New player: 'Sorry about this afternoon, skipper. I've never played this badly before.'

Captain: 'Oh, you have played before, have you?'

The dressing room had an air of gloom and despondency about it as the captain breezed in to give his players a pep-talk. 'All right, lads,' he said cheerfully, 'this is not the time to be superstitious. Just because we've lost the last twelve games doesn't necessarily mean we're going to lose today!'

Slowly the spectator took off his hat and examined it closely. 'I don't believe it!' he exclaimed. 'There are 30,000 spectators in this ground, plus twenty-two players, two linesmen, one referee and the Band of the Welsh Guards – and that damned pigeon has to pick on me!'

'What's this I hear about your not playing for United any more?'

'That's right.'

'Why's that then?'

'It's all down to something the manager said to me.'

'What did he say?'

'You're fired!'

The referee had just awarded a penalty against the visting team. The player who had committed the foul shouted, 'You're the worst ref I ever saw! I think you stink!'

Picking up the ball, the referee walked back a further fifteen yards from the goal. Then he shouted across to the offending player, 'How do I smell from here?'

A keen player left home to take part in a match one Saturday afternoon, only to return an hour later looking very despondent. 'What's the matter, dear?' asked his wife. 'Was the match cancelled?'

'No. I've been dropped from the team,' replied her husband.

'That's terrible! Did they tell you why?'

'Well, all the captain said was that they didn't allow visitors in the dressing room!'

A small local football team had a run of bad luck and had not scored a single goal in six games. The coach called a training session one Saturday morning and said, 'You all seem to have forgotten how to kick! Now just watch me and see if you can learn something.' He placed the ball twenty yards from the goal and kicked. His shot missed the goal completely. He tried a dozen more kicks and every one of them missed the net. Finally he turned to the team and panted, 'That's the sort of thing you lot have been doing! Now let's see if you can't get out there this afternoon and score some goals!'

Two chaps were walking through a cemetery when they saw a tombstone which bore the legend: HERE LIES A FOOTBALL MANAGER AND AN HONEST MAN. One chap turned to the other and said, 'I didn't know they were allowed to bury two fellows in the same grave.'

A fellow turned up at a match last Saturday just before half-time. He said to a young lady sitting next to him, 'Whose game?'

'I am,' she said sweetly.

A teacher in a London comprehensive asked her class to write a short account of a football match. After a couple of minutes one small boy put down his pen. 'You can't have finished already, Billy,' said the teacher in surprise.

'Yes, I have, miss,' said Billy.

'Well, show me what you've written,' said the teacher.

Billy handed over his work. It consisted of just six words: 'Game cancelled on account of rain.'

'What sort of a match was it last Saturday?'
'Terrible! The only people who played well were the band at half-time.'

MacTavish: 'I hear you went over to Aberdeen to see the match last Saturday, Sandy. Was it a big gate?'

MacDonald: 'It was that, Jock! One of the biggest I've ever climbed over!'

'What's your goalkeeper like?'
'Blind as a bat! He can't even see the ball when it's coming straight at him!'
'That's nothing. Ours can't even find it when it's in the net!'

My home town has a great football team. Last season they lost ten games in a row, but were they discouraged? No! They went right out and lost ten more!

One of the England players, who shall be nameless, had made the acquaintance of a young lady in the lobby of the hotel at which he was staying. He invited her to dinner and spent the entire meal regaling her with anecdotes about his prowess on the field, and how he had held the team together in the most crucial games. As coffee was being served, he said, 'But that's enough about me. Let's talk about you. Tell me, what did you think of my game in the match against Italy?'

There's only one difference today between a professional football player and an amateur, according to a cynic of my acquaintance: the professional gets paid by cheque.

A group of flies were playing football in a saucer, using a lump of sugar as a ball. One of them said, 'We'll have to do better than this, lads – we're playing in the cup tomorrow!'

Referees do very well financially at Leeds United matches. They get 5p back on every bottle.

Boss: 'Why are you so late for work?'
Employee: 'Sorry, boss. I dreamed I was watching the Cup Final and it ran into extra time.'

A lucky fellow recently won £250,000 on the football pools and bought a large public-house in south London. He announced his intention of having it completely redecorated from top to bottom, and on the day the work was completed a large crowd gathered outside at opening time. Suddenly the door opened, and there was the pools winner clutching a pint of beer and accompanied by a very curvaceous blonde.

'What time do you open, mate?' shouted a voice from the crowd.

'Open?' said the pools winner. 'What are you talking about? I bought this place for myself!'

Paddy spread the newspaper out on the table and turned the pages until he came to the 'Spot-the-Ball' competition. He studied the picture carefully, then, taking a pin, he proceeded to prick the picture in an orderly manner.

'What are you doing, Paddy?' asked his room-mate, Mick.

'Trying to find the ball,' said Paddy.

'With a pin? How can you do it with a pin?' asked Mick.

'Well, you keep pricking the paper until you hear a hissing noise. Then you know you've punctured the ball, and there you are!'

Two girls were discussing their local football team. 'I've been out with every member of the Rovers and I haven't made love to one of them!' said one.

'Ah!' said her friend. 'I'll bet it was that shy goalkeeper!'

'Was it a good match this afternoon?' one hooligan asked another.

'Yeah – great!' said his mate. 'Ten arrests, three cars wrecked, a running battle with the police and the referee had his arm broken!'

It's said that everyone is football-mad in Scunthorpe. It's quite true, but then they've got a lot to be mad about.

There's a pub near Arsenal's Highbury stadium where every Saturday night, as regular as clockwork, there are scenes of mayhem and bloodshed as the fans discuss the afternoon's match. A local walked in one Sunday lunchtime and said, in surprise, 'Hey, landlord, what's the idea of putting sawdust all over the floor?'

'That's not sawdust,' said the landlord. 'That's Saturday night's furniture.'

A home supporter staggered into a bar after a Cup match between Walsall and visiting Spurs. 'How did it go?' asked the barman.

'Spurs 15, Walsall nil,' gasped the fan. 'And we were damn lucky to get nil!'

First seagull: 'That's Wembley stadium down there – the Cup Final's just started. Look – there's Paul Gascoigne!'
Second seagull: 'Where? I can't see him.'
First seagull: 'Yes, there he is – I'll spot him for you!'

One famous English international was known to his fellow-players as 'V-Neckline'. He was always plunging down the middle but he rarely showed anything interesting.

A Coventry fan, discussing his team in the local, remarked, 'Dobson would be a good player if it weren't for two things.'

'What are those?' asked a bystander.

'His feet!'

I read a report last week of a keen football fan who had his new baby christened Maradona Dalglish Gascoigne Pele. I think the poor girl's going to be in trouble later in life.

'What did the manager say to you last Saturday when you let in three own goals?'

'Shall I leave out the swear words?'

'Yes.'

'He didn't say anything.'

'I hear you were playing football last Sunday, my son.'

'That's right, vicar. It's not a sin to play football on the Sabbath, is it?'

'It is, the way you play it.'

'What did you think of my game today, coach?'

'Not bad – but I still prefer football.'

The village team had finished bottom of the league for the tenth consecutive year, and as two supporters walked away from the last match of the season, one remarked, 'Well, there's one thing you must say about our boys – they're good losers!'

'Good?' exclaimed his friend. 'They're perfect!'

'How was the match, dear?' asked the wife of a football fan who had just returned home.

'The other side won,' he grumbled. 'By seven very lucky goals!'

A leading footballer died and went to Heaven. At the impressive gates an angel checked his record while St Peter chatted to him. 'I see you're a footballer,' said St Peter, 'and judging by your reports, a very good one.'

'Well,' replied the footballer, 'I did represent my country a number of times.'

'I'm sure you'd like to see our football facilities,' went on St Peter. 'Come on – I'll show them to you.'

When they reached the ground the footballer was amazed at the wonderful facilities. A number of players were at practice and one of them was running around busily shouting instructions and giving advice to the others. The footballer said, 'Who does he think he is? God?'

'He *is* God,' whispered St Peter. 'But he thinks he's Paul Gascoigne!'

The selection committee members were discussing the performances of their players. 'Now we come to the goalkeeper, Nick Fanshawe,' said the chairman. 'What are your views on him?'

'As a goalkeeper,' snorted one member, 'I think Venus de Milo could do a better job!'

'It's obvious why we got beaten last Saturday. The referee comes from the same town as the visiting team.'

'Well, it's only natural, then, isn't it? He's got to travel back in the same train with them.'

An avid football fan turned up at a match between Falkirk and Raith Rovers and proffered £3 to the ticket-seller. 'It's £6 to get in,' said the clerk.

'That's all right,' said the Scotsman. 'I'm a Falkirk supporter – I'll only be watching me own lads!'

A very keen football supporter visited a psychiatrist who was also a fanatical follower of the game. 'I'm going to give you an idea-association test,' said the psychiatrist. 'Now tell me – what is it that has smooth curves and tends to become uncontrollable at crucial moments?'

'A football,' said the patient.

'Good! And what do you think of when two arms slip around your waist?'

'An illegal tackle.'

'Excellent! And what sort of picture comes into your mind

at the mention of a pair of round firm thighs?'

'A World Cup footballer.'

'Very good indeed! Your reactions are perfectly normal. But I'll tell you one thing – you'd be surprised at some of the silly answers I get!'

A very noisy home supporter kept disagreeing vociferously with every decision the referee made. In the end the ref couldn't stand it any longer. He marched over to the stands and shouted up at the offender, 'Who's refereeing this match – you or me?'

'Neither of us!' came the prompt reply.

The
World's Best
After-Dinner
Jokes

The proud young mother was discussing with her husband what they should call the new baby. 'I've made up my mind,' she declared firmly. 'We'll call her Penelope.' The husband didn't like the name at all, but he decided to be subtle about it.

'That's a lovely name, dear,' he said. 'The first girl I ever went out with was called Penelope and it will bring back pleasant memories.'

'I think we'll call her Mary, after my mother,' said the wife.

A businessman decided to take the afternoon off and got home about three o'clock in the afternoon. The house was quiet and he went upstairs and opened the bedroom door. His wife was in bed and there was a strange man lying on top of her with his head between her breasts. 'What the hell are you doing?' he shouted.

The man looked up and said, 'I'm listening to the music.'

'What music?' said the husband, and he leaned over and put his ear to his wife's chest. 'I can't hear any music,' he said suspiciously.

'Of course you can't,' said the stranger. 'You're not plugged in.'

A schoolteacher asked her class to write an essay on the subject of the Police. One boy's essay consisted of just three words: 'Police is bastards.'

The teacher was, naturally, shocked, and she arranged for her class to visit the local police station so that they could meet the policemen and find out how they worked. The police were most co-operative and the children had a great day out, listening in to the radio calls, riding around in panda cars and inspecting the police station, the whole thing topped off with a slap-up tea.

Back at school the next day, the teacher again asked the class to write an essay on the police, based on their experiences. This time the lad's essay consisted of the following: 'Police is cunning bastards.'

A prominent City banker fell in love with an actress and for several weeks, he took her out and about to all the fashionable nightclubs and restaurants. Deciding to ask her to marry him, he prudently engaged a firm of private detectives to check her antecedents, since any hint of scandal might jeopardize his position in the City.

In due course, he received their report: 'Miss Delamere appears to have led a blameless existence, and there are no indications of promiscuity, drugs, or criminal activities. Her friends and acquaintances are similarly beyond reproach. The only thing we have been able to discover about her is that, in recent weeks, she has been seen around in the company of a City banker of doubtful reputation.'

A suburbanite rang up a friend of his to invite him to a party. 'You know the address, don't you?' he said. 'You can't miss it — when you get to the town hall, take the second turning on the left, and we're the fourth house along. Just ring the bell with your elbow.'

'Why my elbow?' said his friend.

'Well, you're not coming empty-handed, are you?' he said.

The club bore was talking about his travels in India. 'I remember on one occasion,' he said, 'in a little village on the banks of the Ganges, a number of the women were washing clothes when a large tiger appeared from nowhere. One of the women immediately splashed some water in its face, and do you know, that tiger turned round and slunk back into the jungle!'

There was a moment's silence and then another club member said, 'I can vouch for the truth of that incident. I was there myself. As I was coming down to the river, I came face to face with the tiger and I stroked its whiskers. Gentlemen, those whiskers were wet!'

A doting mother, who wanted desperately to see her 23-year-old daughter happily married, decided to help matters along by putting an advertisement in the local paper. After careful consideration, she submitted the following to the Lonely Hearts Column: *Lonely, unattached red-head, 23, good figure, fun-loving, uninhibited, seeks male company.*

A few days later, the daughter asked her mother whether there had been any replies. 'Just one,' said her mother grimly. 'From your father!'

The cute little secretary walked into her boss's office one morning and said, 'I have some good news and some bad news for you.'

'Look, I'm very busy this morning,' said the boss. 'Just tell me the good news.'

'Well,' said the secretary, 'the good news is that you're not sterile.'

The hotel lobby was crowded as the receptionist shouted, 'Is there a Mr Hausenburgenkranzermacher here? I have an urgent message for Mr Hausenburgenkranzermacher.'

A bespectacled gent looked up from his newspaper and said, 'What initial?'

At the weekly meeting of the Women's Institute, one of the members was enthusing about the recent First Aid course she had attended. 'It was a lucky thing I went on that course,' she said. 'I was coming down the High Street yesterday when I heard a big crash behind me. I looked round and there was this poor chap who'd been knocked down by a taxi. He was covered in blood, and he looked to have a broken arm and a compound fracture of the leg – and possibly a fractured skull. And then I remembered what I had learned on my First Aid course. So I bent over and put my head between my legs to stop myself from fainting.'

Shortly after the German invasion of Belgium in 1940, a Panzer regiment occupied a small town near the frontier. The commanding officer of the German troops assembled all the inhabitants in the town hall and instructed them to take an oath of allegiance to the Third Reich. One man refused indignantly and boasted of the brave defence the Belgian army had put up against the invading Nazi hordes. The German was outraged and shouted, 'Unless you take this oath of allegiance, you will be taken outside and shot!'

Bowing to the inevitable, the Belgian took the oath and

the officer said, 'That's better! Now you are one of us!'

The Belgian looked at him and said, 'Fine! But didn't those Belgians give us a hell of a fight!'

Two ex-army men met in a pub and began to talk over old times in the service. 'You remember I used to be in the band?' said one. 'Well, I used to play the trumpet, and I married a girl who plays the piano. We've got two children – a boy who plays the drums, and a girl who's a dab hand with the guitar. Tell you what – pop over one evening and we'll give you a little musical concert.'

'I'll do that,' said his pal. 'I used to box for the regiment and I married a girl who's got a black belt at judo. My boy's a policeman and does a bit of wrestling on the side. You must come round to us one evening – we can't give you a musical concert but we'll give you a bloody good hiding!'

Groucho Marx was leaving a particularly boring Hollywood party. At the door, he said to the hostess, 'I've had a wonderful evening – but this wasn't it.'

A man went to see his solicitor and asked if he could have his wife traced. They had been married twenty-five years ago and had split up just three days after the wedding. The solicitor asked him why he had waited so long – was he thinking of a divorce? 'No,' said the man. 'I just thought we might get together to celebrate our Silver Anniversary.'

A woman went to a psychiatrist and said, 'It's my husband, doctor. He thinks he's a lift.'

'Well, why don't you ask him to call in and see me?' said the psychiatrist.

'He can't,' said the wife. 'He doesn't stop at this floor.'

'What happened?' asked the hospital visitor of the heavily bandaged man sitting up in bed.

'Well, I went down to Margate at the weekend and decided to take a ride on the roller coaster. As we came up to the top of the highest loop, I noticed a little sign by the side of the track. I tried to read it but it was very small and I couldn't make it out. I was so curious that I decided to go round again, but we went by so quickly that I couldn't see what the sign said. By now, I was determined to read that sign so I went round a third time. As we reached the top, I stood up in the car to get a better view.'

'And did you manage to see what the sign said this time?' asked the visitor.

'Yes.'

'What did it say?'

'Don't stand up in the car!'

A holiday-maker wrote to a hotel in Devon asking if it was all right for his dog to stay there too. The hotel owner wrote back: *Dear Sir, I have been running this hotel for fifteen years. Never once in all that time has a dog set the bedclothes on fire by smoking in bed. I have never found hotel towels in a dog's suitcase, or had a dog attempt to pass off a bad cheque on me. Your dog is welcome — and if he can vouch for you, you can come too.*

Arthur Sullivan, of Gilbert and Sullivan fame, was reputed to have perfect pitch. One night, he stumbled home after a late party, considerably the worse for drink. He had difficulty in identifying his house from all the other identical houses in the street so he went down the row kicking at the metal shoe-scrapers by the side of each flight of steps. Eventually he came to one and kicked it, then paused and kicked it again. 'Ah! E flat!' he muttered. 'This must be the one.'

A young married couple were having a furious argument. 'I wish now that I'd taken my mother's advice and never married you!' sobbed the bride.

'Do you mean to tell me,' said the husband incredulously, 'that your mother tried to stop you marrying me?'

'Yes, she did,' said the wife.

'Good God!' the husband exclaimed. 'How I've wronged that woman!'

A woman went to her doctor for a check-up and he said, 'You've been married three times, haven't you?'

'Yes,' she said.

'And yet you're still a virgin?' said the doctor.

'Yes,' she replied. 'You see, my first husband was a homosexual. My second was ninety-three years old. And my third was in public relations. All he did was sit on my bed and tell me how wonderful it was going to be.'

A fellow on a Mediterranean cruise was invited by the captain to take a look around the bridge. 'This is a first-class ship,' the captain told him. 'The crew are all hand-picked. Every man is an expert at his job. You see that fellow down there, swabbing the deck? He's a typical example. I would trust that man with my life.' Just then a huge wave dashed over the ship and swept the sailor overboard.

'You know that feller you said you'd trust with your life?' said the passenger. 'Well, he's just done a bunk with your mop and bucket!'

A woman rang up a vet in the small hours and complained that a dog and a bitch were copulating noisily at the bottom of her garden. Could he do anything about it? 'Madam,' said the vet, 'it's half past two in the morning and you've got me out of bed. Why don't you try telling those dogs that they're wanted on the phone?'

'Do you think that will stop them?' asked the woman.

'Well, it certainly stopped me,' said the vet.

An old lady from the West Country had reached her hundredth birthday and was being interviewed on television. 'You look in remarkably good health,' said the interviewer. 'Have you ever been bedridden?'

'Oh, yes,' she answered. 'Lots of times. And once in a hansom cab!'

A Dublin lawyer was defending a client who was being sued for returning a borrowed lawn mower in a damaged condition. 'Your Honour,' said the lawyer, 'we refute this charge on the following grounds. In the first place, my client never borrowed the lawn mower at all. In the second place, it was already damaged when he borrowed it. And in the third place, it was in perfect condition when he returned it.'

Two friends were chatting in the saloon bar and one said, 'No matter what kind of girl I bring home to meet my parents, my mother disapproves of her.'

'I'll tell you what to do,' said his friend. 'Find a girl just like your mother. She's bound to like her.'

A week later, the two friends met again. 'Did you do what I advised?' asked the second fellow.

'Yes, I did,' replied the first. 'I found a girl who was just like my mother – even dressed and talked like her.'

'So what happened when you took her home?'

'My father hated her!'

Orson Welles was once lecturing in a small town in Kansas. Only a handful of people turned up to hear him and he looked round at the half-dozen people in the audience and said, 'My name is Orson Welles. I am an actor, a writer, a director and a producer. I am also a painter and a magician, and I play the piano and the violin. Isn't it a pity there are so many of me and so few of you!'

A prospective parliamentary candidate had just finished a long speech in the local hall of a small town in the north of England. Feeling very pleased with himself for having delivered a rousing, fact-filled and inspiring speech, he said, 'Are there any questions?'

'Yes,' said a bored voice from the back. 'Who else is running?'

George Bernard Shaw once sent Winston Churchill a couple of tickets for the opening night of one of his plays. Attached to the tickets was a note: *Bring a friend − if you have one.*

Churchill was busy that evening, so he returned the tickets to Shaw with a note which read: *Can't make tonight. I'll come to the second performance − if there is one.*

A millionaire businessman once commissioned a French artist to paint his wife's picture. At the first sitting, the wife said to the Frenchman, 'I know I am not a great beauty, and I would like a true likeness, but please, Monsieur, may I ask that you paint me with sympathy.'

After some weeks the portrait was finished and the husband arranged a grand unveiling ceremony. The cover was drawn back from the portrait and the assembled guests gasped in horror. It was a wonderful likeness but the picture showed a man's hand reaching into the lady's bosom. The husband was furious. 'How dare you insult my wife in this fashion!' he stormed.

'But, Monsieur, I do not understand,' protested the

Frenchman. 'Your wife asked me to paint her with sympathy. I did not know what "sympathy" meant so I looked it up in the dictionary. It said, "Sympathy — a fellow feeling in your bosom." '

An Irishman was fishing when suddenly he heard a voice from overhead. 'There are no fish under the ice!' the voice boomed.

The Irishman dropped his rod in a panic and said in a trembling voice, 'Is that you, God?'

'No,' thundered the voice. 'I'm the manager of the ice rink!'

A psychiatrist interviewing a patient said, 'I want to try some free association. Just answer the following questions as quickly as you can — just say the first thing that comes into your head. Now, first — what is it that a man does standing up, a lady sitting down, and a dog on three legs?'

'Shakes hands,' said the patient at once.

'Good,' said the psychiatrist. 'Now what is it that a dog does in the garden that you wouldn't want to step in?'

'Digs a hole,' said the patient without hesitation.

'Right,' said the psychiatrist. 'And, finally, what is it that sticks stiffly out of your pyjamas when you wake up in the morning?'

'Your head,' said the patient.

'Excellent,' said the psychiatrist. 'Your responses are perfectly normal — but you'd be surprised at some of the weird answers I get!'

An American was complaining to an Englishman in the Savoy Grill that he found many English terms confusing. 'You say "rubbish" and we say "garbage",' he explained. 'We say "elevator" and you say "lift"; you say "dustbin" and we say "trash can". And then there's your pronunciation – I can't make head or tail of that.'

'Surely that shouldn't give you any problems?' said the Englishman. 'There can't be that much difference.'

'Oh yeah?' said the American. 'Why, only the other day, I was walking down Drury Lane and I passed a theatre with a big sign saying, "CATS – pronounced success!"'

A man on a Caribbean cruise was standing on the deck one night, admiring the moonlit waters, when another passenger approached, pulled out a small container from his pocket, and sprinkled the contents over the water. 'Those are my wife's ashes,' he explained.

'I see,' said the first man. 'You must have loved her very much.'

'No,' said the second man. 'I hate fish.'

A very devout rabbi, deeply engrossed in his meditations, had a vision in which he imagined that he saw God himself. 'You look worried,' said God. 'Is anything the matter?'

'Oh, God, it's my son,' the rabbi said. 'He's about to become a Christian!'

And God said, '*Your* son!'

A mother took her three-year-old son to a psychiatrist and explained that she was worried that he was becoming too precocious. 'Right,' said the psychiatrist, 'we'll try a few simple tests.' Turning to the boy, he said, 'Just say a few words – anything that comes into your mind.'

The boy turned to his mother and said, 'Does he want logically constructed sentences or just random and purely isolated words?'

A young lady approached a gentleman at a Mayfair party and said, 'Do you remember me? A few years ago, you asked me to marry you.'

'And did I?' replied the man.

An Irish detective arrested a wanted criminal in a Dublin street. Just as he was about to slap the handcuffs on him, a gust of wind blew the detective's hat down the street. 'Shall I go and fetch it for you?' asked the criminal.

'Do you think I'm crazy?' said the detective. 'You wait here and I'll go and get it.'

A visitor to an Indian reservation in Oklahoma met a Comanche chief on the top of a mountain. The chief was squatting by a small fire and sending out smoke signals. Having an interest in Indian customs, the visitor asked, 'How big a fire do you usually build?'

'Well,' said the Indian, 'that depends on whether it's a local or a long-distance call.'

An examiner marking papers at Cambridge came across the following answer to one of the mathematics questions: 'God only knows the answer to this one.' He returned the paper with the notation: 'God gets an A. You get an F.'

'Doctor,' said the patient, 'I had a peculiar dream last night. I dreamed you were my mother.'
'So?' said the psychiatrist. 'What happened?'
'Nothing – I woke up.'
'And then?'
'I had breakfast.'
'And what did you have for breakfast?'
'Oh, just a piece of toast and a cup of coffee.'
'Call that a breakfast?' said the psychiatrist.

At the height of his popularity, Rudyard Kipling was earning quite a lot of money. An American admirer once wrote to him, saying, 'They tell me that you get $1 a word from your writing. I enclose a dollar for which please send me a sample.'
Kipling replied. 'Thanks.'
Soon afterwards, he received another letter from the American: 'I sold the "Thanks" anecdote for $2. Enclosed pleased find 45 cents being half the profits from the transaction, less postage.'

An English tourist arrived in Cairo. As soon as he set foot on Egyptian soil, a pimp came up to him and said, 'You want nice little virgin, nine years old?'

'Of course not!' said the visitor.

'How about very pretty little boy, ten years old, also virgin?'

'Get away from here!' said the tourist, outraged. 'I don't want a little girl or a little boy! I want the British Consul!'

'Hmmm,' murmured the pimp. 'Very difficult – but I try.'

On a visit to Brighton, a lady went into a fortune-teller's tent. After the customary crossing of the palm with silver, the clairvoyant said, 'I see a bright future for you. You will meet a tall, dark, handsome man. He will be very rich. You will marry him and he will take you off to a life of luxury. You will have everything your heart desires.'

'Sounds great,' said the lady. 'Just one question . . .'

'Ask away,' said the fortune-teller.

'How do I get rid of my husband?'

A young girl visiting Paris was propositioned by a Frenchman and eventually succumbed to his advances. She was very surprised, however, when he insisted on having her against a wall instead of in bed. Afterwards, she asked him why. 'All Frenchmen know,' he explained, 'that the English are always at their best when their backs are against the wall.'

An Irish disc jockey was introducing a record. 'This next one,' he said, 'is for Mr Michael O'Reilly, who is a hundred and eleven. Well done, Michael, that's a ripe old age, isn't it!' There was a short pause, and then the disc jockey said, 'I'm sorry, I got that wrong. This next record is for Michael O'Reilly, who is ill.'

The visitor was complaining to the landlady. 'Your advertisement claimed that your hotel was only ten minutes from the sea,' he said. 'It took me forty-five minutes to get there this morning.'

'Ah,' said the landlady, 'you've been walking. We don't cater for pedestrians.'

Some people seem to be phenomenally unlucky. Like the young unmarried girl who one day found herself pregnant. Wishing to avoid a scandal in the rather strait-laced community in which she lived, she announced that she was going off on holiday. She travelled to another city at the other end of the country and registered in a small private hospital using a false name. She didn't write home or telephone or tell any of her friends or family where she was. And then she gave birth to quintuplets.

A fellow came ashore outside Calais having swum the Channel in record time. There was a big crowd waiting to greet him and one of the Frenchmen said, 'Magnifique! You 'ave performed the great foot!'

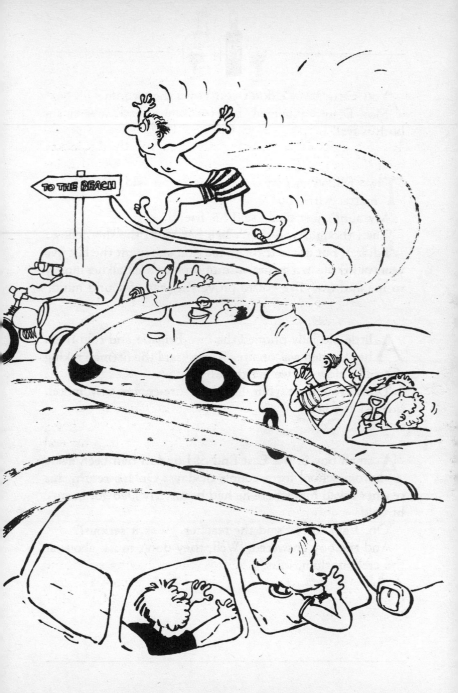

TO THE BEACH

'You mean "feat", don't you?' said the swimmer.

'Mon Dieu!' exclaimed the Frenchman. 'You 'ave swum both ways?'

Two fellows met in the pub and one said, 'What's the matter with you?'

'My aunt's just died,' said his friend.

'But I thought you didn't like her,' said the first fellow.

'I didn't, but it was through me that she spent the last five years of her life in a mental institution. She's left all her money to me and now I've got to prove she was of sound mind.'

A little old lady phoned the Fire Brigade and told them her kitchen was on fire. 'Right,' said the fireman taking the call. 'How do we get there?'

'Don't you have your little red fire-engine any more?' queried the lady.

A small boy in the East End of London had been away from school for a couple of days. On his return, his teacher asked him where he had been. 'My Dad got burnt,' he said.

'Oh, I am sorry,' said the teacher. 'Was it serious?'

And the boy answered, 'Well, they don't muck about at the crematorium, miss!'

In a little village in northern Italy, the priest was addressing the villagers in the local church. 'You must not use-a the Pill!' he exhorted.

A young signorina stepped forward and said indignantly, 'Hey! You no play-a da game, you no make-a da rules!'

When British Rail were planning their new route from central London to the coast, they wrote to a farmer advising him that the proposed line would run right through the middle of his barn. They offered him very good compensation amounting to ten times as much as the property was worth, so it came as something of a shock to his wife when he turned the offer down. 'It's a good offer!' she exclaimed. 'Why don't you take it?'

'No!' he said. 'Do you think I'm going to keep running out to that barn day and night to open and shut the door every time they want to run a train through it?'

A young lady went into Boston's most exclusive department store and made her way to the Ladies' Fashions department. She tried on several dresses and each time, she slipped the dress on, sat down, separated her legs, and said, 'This won't do.' The middle-aged saleswoman was rather shocked and complained to the floor manager. He came over and told the young lady that perhaps it might be better if she left. The young lady said coldly, 'Sir, you have just insulted the principal cellist of the Boston Symphony Orchestra!'

The War Office recently received delivery of a brand-new computer, incorporating the very latest technological improvements. The Commander-in-Chief Home Forces arranged a tactical defence exercise in order to test the computer's capabilities. All the information about our forces and the enemy's was fed into the machine and then the C-in-C asked, 'How do I start the exercise, Computer? Do I attack or do I fight a defensive action?'

The computer replied, 'Yes.'

'Yes, what?' the C-in-C asked impatiently.

'Yes, *sir!*' said the computer.

It was the beginning of term at a primary school in South London. The teacher asked one little Indian boy his name and he replied, 'Ravashanka Vankatarataam Bannerjee.'

'How do you spell that?' she asked.

'My mother helps me,' said the boy.

A young lad obtained a job at a petrol station, wiping windscreens and generally helping out. One day, a very flash Mercedes pulled in, driven by a world-class golf pro. The driver went inside to make a telephone call, and while the young lad was cleaning the car windows he noticed some golf tees on the top of the dashboard. He knew absolutely nothing about golf, so when the pro returned, he asked him what they were for. 'They're to put my balls on when I'm driving,' said the pro.

'Blimey!' said the kid. 'These Mercedes people think of everything, don't they!'

At an Officer's Initiative Course at Sandhurst, the question was put to one group: 'Your platoon is under attack and the situation is desperate. Suddenly, one of the men panics, drops his rifle and runs past you to the rear. The other men look at you in despair. What action would you take?'

One of the officers wrote: 'I would shout "Henderson, hurry back with that ammunition!"'

One Sunday morning, Mark Twain attended a service at which the sermon was preached by Dr Doane, Bishop of Albany. At the end of the service, Twain said, 'A good sermon, Doctor, but you know, I have a book at home which contains every word of it.'

'Impossible!' said the Doctor. 'If there really is such a book, I would very much like to see it.'

The next day, Twain sent him a copy of a dictionary.

Two old ladies were making their very first flight in Concorde. As the stewardess came round to ask if there was anything they wanted, one of the ladies said, 'Please ask the pilot not to travel faster than sound. We want to talk.'

At a recent auction at Sotheby's, the auctioneer said, 'I must interrupt the sale for a moment, gentlemen. A buyer has lost a wallet containing £5,000. He has offered a reward of £300 for its return.'

And a voice from the back of the room shouted, '£350!'

'Did you have a good day at the office, dear?' asked the young wife.

'No,' replied the husband. 'The computer broke down and we all had to think.'

A well-known actress complained to a photographer the pictures he had taken of her made her look too old, and weren't half as good as the ones he had taken some years earlier. 'You must remember,' he explained, 'that I am ten years older than I was on the last occasion I worked for you.'

During the recent Gulf War, a fellow seeking a bit of adventure went into an army recruiting office to sign up. The recruiting officer said, 'What experience do you have? Do you have any war records?'

'Yes, as a matter of fact, I've got two,' said the fellow. 'A Gracie Fields and a Vera Lynn.'

British Rail have a report form that must be completed whenever there is an incident on the line. On one occasion, a driver was filling out the form after accidentally killing a cow on the tracks. In the section devoted to accidents of this kind, there was a section marked 'Disposition of Carcass'. After considerable thought, he wrote: 'Kind and gentle.'

Adam noticed that the animals were often wandering off into the forest in pairs and re-emerging some time later with contented smiles on their faces. He asked Eve about it and she said, 'Don't you know? It's called reproduction.'

The next time he spoke to God, Adam asked, 'What's reproduction?'

'Why don't you take Eve into the woods and find out,' said the Lord.

Adam tried this, but the next time he spoke to God, he asked, 'Lord – what's a headache?'

There was a big murder trial in Iceland recently. At one point, counsel for the prosecution is alleged to have asked a witness, 'Will you please tell the court where you were on the night of the 10th of November to the 6th of March.'

Little Johnny disgraced himself at the dinner table by announcing loudly that he was going for a wee-wee. 'Don't say that, Johnny,' said his shocked mother. 'In future, if you want to go to the toilet, try to be more discreet. Just say, "I want to whisper." '

The next day, little Johnny's grandfather came for a visit. That night at dinner, as Granddad was drinking his soup, Johnny said, 'Excuse me, Granddad – I want to whisper.'

'All right,' said Granddad. 'Come over here and whisper in my ear.'

A small boy accompanied his parents to a nudist colony. They all stripped off and went out into the garden. The boy looked around with interest and then asked his father why 'some men had big ones and some had small ones'. Dad couldn't be bothered with long explanations so he just said, 'Those with big ones are smart and those with small ones are stupid.'

The boy wandered off on his own for a while and then met his father again. 'Have you seen your mother?' asked Dad.

'She's behind that bush over there,' said the boy, 'talking to a stupid man who's getting smarter by the minute.'

The following is the text of a letter said to have been received by an income tax official in Nigeria:

DEAR SIR,

With reference to the attached form. I do not know what is meant by filling in this form. I am not interested in this income service. Please cancel my name in your books as this system has upset my mind and I do not know who registered me as one of your customers.

The lady of the manor at a large stately home in Lincolnshire wrote to the commander of a nearby American air base inviting him to send a dozen airmen round to afternoon tea. She added a PS: 'Please don't send any Jews.'

On the appointed afternoon, her door-bell rang promptly at four o'clock. She opened the door to find twelve black airmen standing on the steps. 'Oh!' she said in confusion, 'there must be some mistake!'

'No, ma'am,' said the airman in charge of the party. 'Captain Cohen never makes mistakes.'

A very keen amateur gardener was very proud of his ferns, the fronds of which were particularly fine specimens. He decided to try his hand at anemones but the results were a disaster. He complained to his friend. 'My fronds are absolute perfection,' he said, 'but I just can't grow anemones.'

'Never mind,' replied his friend. 'With fronds like these, who needs anemones!'

A young girl whose job it was to sell cosmetics by telephone, called one number and when a male voice answered, asked to speak to his wife. 'I'm afraid my wife is dying and can't speak to anyone,' replied the man sadly.

'Oh, I am sorry,' said the girl.

And the voice replied, 'So am I. I wanted her to stay brunette.'

A fellow was cleaning out his attic one morning when he came across an old brass lamp. He gave it a rub and a genie appeared in a puff of smoke. 'I am the genie of the lamp,' said the apparition. 'For releasing me, I will answer any three questions you care to ask.'

'Who? Me?' said the young man.

'Yes, you,' replied the genie. 'Now, what's your third question?'

'It seems there were these two Jews . . .' a comedian said as he started his routine in a northern club.

Immediately, a fellow stood up and shouted, 'Just a minute! I'm Jewish – why are you always knocking Jewish people like this? Every other joke you hear these days starts off "There were these two Jews . . ." '

'Sorry,' said the comedian. 'No need to take offence. I'll start again. There were these two Chinese, Lee Chan and Fu Ching, on their way over to the synagogue for a barmitzvah . . .'

'I'm sorry,' said the gynaecologist, after completing his examination, 'but removing that vibrator is going to involve a very delicate operation.

'Well,' said the young lady, 'couldn't you just change the batteries?'

During a naval exercise in the Mediterranean, a signaller rushed up to the bridge and said, 'Captain, this message just came in.'

'Read it out,' said the captain.

'Well, sir, I . . .' the signalman stammered.

'Just read it out – now!' snapped the captain.

'Right, sir,' said the signalman. 'It reads: *What the hell do you think you're doing, you stupid, blundering idiot? You're not fit to be in command!*'

'Yes, well . . .' said the captain. 'Have that decoded at once.'

An MP decided to take up ballooning. On his first trip, the weather took a turn for the worse and the balloon was forced down into a field miles from anywhere. As the mist closed in, the MP realized that he was completely lost. Just then, he noticed a farmer crossing the field and he shouted, 'Can you tell me where I am?'

'You're in a balloon!' the farmer shouted back, and carried on walking.

Recounting this incident to his colleagues in the bar of the House of Commons the next day, the MP said, 'That farmer gave me the perfect parliamentary reply. It was short. It was true. And it gave absolutely no new information.'

Two married couples made up a foursome for an evening of contract bridge. One of the husbands was a terrible player and his wife became progressively more annoyed as they lost hand after hand. Eventually, the husband excused himself to go to the bathroom, and his wife remarked, 'This is the first time all evening that I know what he has in his hand.'

Having finished his dinner, a man was leaving a West End restaurant. The owner of the restaurant was standing in the doorway, and as the man passed him a solid silver sugar bowl slipped out from under his bulging jacket and dropped to the floor with a resounding crash. With great presence of mind, the man looked round and said indignantly, 'Who threw that?'

A famous violinist became very interested in the effect of classical music on wild animals. He went out to Africa and took his violin into the heart of the jungle. Then he took out his violin and started to play a beautiful piece by Paganini. A huge gorilla approached and sat down entranced. He was followed by a fierce-looking bull elephant and a twenty-foot boa constrictor, both of whom stopped to listen to the music with dreamy expressions on their faces. Soon the violinist was surrounded by a group of normally ferocious animals, all listening, fascinated, to the music. Then an old lion bounded up, leaped on the violinist and tore him to pieces. 'What the hell did you do that for?' cried the gorilla. 'Our first chance to listen to really good music and you go and ruin it!'

And the lion cupped his paw to his ear and said, 'Pardon?'

The vicar of a small parish in a West Country town had a horseshoe hanging over his front door. 'I'm surprised to see a horseshoe up there,' said one of his parishioners. 'I didn't know you believed in these pagan superstitions. Do you really think it will bring you luck?'

'No, I'm not really superstitious,' said the vicar. 'But I have been told that it works even if you don't believe in it.'

The school governor was addressing a class of sixth-form girls at the end of the school year. 'Now, remember, girls,' he said, 'you are the mothers and wives of tomorrow!'

'It was through getting things in that order,' muttered the headmistress, 'that we had to expel Susie Simpkins!'

Two Irish astronauts landed on the moon and one of them left the spaceship to take a walk round the lunar landscape, leaving the other one to prepare for the journey home. After about half an hour, there was a knock on the door of the spaceship. The second astronaut looked up and said, 'Who's there?'

A woman went into a butcher's shop to buy a chicken. The butcher produced the last chicken he had for sale that day and the woman said, 'Have you got one a little bigger?'

'Just a minute,' said the butcher and he disappeared with the chicken into the back room, where he plumped up the bird so that it looked bigger. Returning into the shop, he put it down on the counter and said, 'How about this?'

'Fine,' said the woman. 'I'll take both of them.'

A honeymoon couple entered the lift at their hotel. As the lift ascended, one of the other guests, a very attractive young girl, looked at the groom and said, 'Hello, darling!'

When they reached their bedroom, the new bride said icily, 'And just who was that in the lift?'

'Don't you start!' said the groom. 'I'll have enough trouble explaining you to her!'

A little boy returning home from his first day at school said to his mother, 'Mum, what's sex?' His mother, who believed in all the most modern educational theories, gave him a detailed explanation, covering all aspects of the tricky subject. When she had finished, the little lad produced an enrolment form which he had brought home from school and said, 'Yes, but how am I going to get all that into this one little square?'

A woman whose husband had just joined the Navy attended church one Sunday morning. She only just got there in time and she hurriedly handed the vicar a note, asking if he would read it out in the pulpit. The note read: *Norman Smith having gone to sea, his wife desires the prayers of the congregation for his safety.*

The minister, in a hurry, took the note and went up into the pulpit. When the time came for him to read the notices, he glanced quickly at the note and said, 'Norman Smith, having gone to see his wife, desires the prayers of the congregation for his safety.'

The local church was putting on a nativity play and the vicar went up to London to order a banner from a firm of printers. Unfortunately he lost the note he had made of the dimensions of the banner and the Bible quotation to be printed on it, so he sent a fax message to his wife, asking her to confirm the details. He went out to lunch whilst awaiting the reply and when this came through it was taken by one of the clerks in the printing firm. The poor girl nearly fainted when she read the message: *Unto us a child is born — eight feet long and three feet wide.*

An East End trader who euphemistically described himself as being in 'imports and exports' fell foul of the Inland Revenue and was summoned for an interview. 'It seems from our records,' said the inspector, 'that you have not filed any returns for eight years. According to our calculations, you owe a total of £30,000 in back taxes, and I must request immediate payment, otherwise we shall have to issue the usual summons.'

'That's fair enough,' said the trader, and he opened a large suitcase which he had with him, and produced £30,000 in used notes.

The surprised tax man counted the money and said, 'Well, that seems to be in order – I'll just give you a receipt.'

'A receipt!' gasped the trader. 'Thirty thousand nicker in cash and you're going to put it through the books!'

The great chess master Bobby Fischer was travelling through the southern states of America and booked in one night at a small town in the backwoods of Alabama. The proprietor had no idea who he was and asked him in the course of the evening if he would like to play a game of chess. Being Fischer, he did not reveal his identity, but agreed to play. To his amazement, the hotel proprietor wiped the floor with him in seventeen moves – and without using his rooks. 'This is incredible!' Fischer said. 'And you never even used your rooks!'

'Oh, you mean those pieces at each end shaped like little castles?' said the hotel proprietor. 'No – I never did figure out how they moved.'

A door-to-door salesman knocked at the door of a typical suburban house in Wimbledon. 'Good morning,' he said. 'Would you care to buy a copy of *Five Hundred Excuses To Give Your Wife For Staying Out Late?*'

'Why on earth would I want a book like that?' said the lady of the house.

'Because,' replied the salesman, 'I sold a copy to your husband at his office this morning.'

An Irishman, an Italian and a Jew were regaling each other with stories about how they were continually being mistaken for famous historical figures. 'Oh, yes,' said the Irishman. 'Why I was walking through the park the other day and a fellow shouted "Morning, Saint Patrick!" '

The Italian said, 'I was standing on the street corner yesterday and a man passed by and said, "Hello, Mussolini!" '

The Jew said, 'That's nothing. I was walking through the park this morning and a policeman shouted, "Jesus Christ, get off the grass!" '

A fellow staying at a seaside boarding house sat down to dinner on his first evening and the dog growled at him. 'What's the matter with him?' the fellow asked.

'You've got his plate,' said the landlady.

'Well, I hope he makes friends,' said the guest nervously.

'So do I,' said the landlady. 'You're sleeping with him tonight.'

A young husband came home from the office one evening and found his wife in tears. 'Darling, the most terrible thing has happened!' she sobbed. 'The first casserole I ever made for you and the cat ate it!'

'Don't worry, darling,' said the husband. 'I'll get you another cat tomorrow.'

It was a teenage marriage. The groom was seventeen. The bride was sixteen, going on pregnant. When the vicar asked the bridegroom to repeat after him: 'With all my worldly goods I thee endow,' the groom's mother turned to her husband and whispered, 'There goes his paper round!'

The Germans had just occupied Paris, and on the day of their arrival, a young French girl was raped by a German soldier. Afterwards, he said to her, 'In nine months, you will have a son – you may call him Adolf.'

She replied, 'In nine days, you will have a rash – you may call it measles.'

A lovely young thing was walking down the King's Road in Chelsea, wearing the tightest pair of jeans you ever saw. A young man approached her and said, 'I hope you don't mind my asking, but how on earth does anyone get into those pants?'

'Well,' she said, 'you could start by buying me a Martini.'

A fellow received a 'Second Notice' from the tax authorities informing him that his tax payment was overdue and threatening legal action if settlement was not immediately forthcoming. He hurried down to the collector's office and wrote out a cheque, saying, 'I would have paid you before but I didn't get your First Notice.'

'Oh,' said the clerk, 'we've run out of First Notices – and anyway, we find that the Second Notices are far more effective.'

The headmaster of a school in South London asked the father of one of his pupils to pop in for a chat. When the father arrived in his office, the headmaster said, 'I'm afraid this is serious. It's about your son, Jimmy.'

'What's he been up to now?' asked the father.

'Well, yesterday, we caught him having a wee in the swimming pool.'

'Well, that's not so bad, is it?' said the father. 'All little boys have an occasional wee in the swimming pool.'

'I know,' said the headmaster. 'But not from the top diving board!'

A professor of biology was lecturing to his class on the subject of cause and effect. He placed a flea on the desk in front of him and ordered it to jump. The flea jumped. Then he picked the flea up and cut off its legs. Placing it back on the desk, he again ordered it to jump. The flea didn't move. 'This demonstrates conclusively,' he said, 'that when the legs of a flea are removed, it is rendered completely deaf.'

A young married couple decided it would be a good idea if they made their wills. Returning from the solicitor's office, the husband said, 'I'm glad we did that, darling. If anything happened to me, I'd want you to get married again. I only ask one thing: if you did, don't let him wear my clothes.'

'Oh, no,' replied the wife. 'Anyway, they wouldn't fit him.'

Father had decided that the time had come when he should explain the facts of life to his teenage son. He called the lad into his living-room one morning and spent the next hour explaining in great detail everything he knew of the sexual process. Utterly exhausted, and not wishing to go through the whole business again with his younger son, he said, 'Now, David, can I rely on you to explain everything to Michael?'

'Sure, Dad,' said the teenager. 'Leave it to me.'

That afternoon, David took Michael aside and said, 'Micky, I had a long lecture from Dad this morning and he wants me to pass on to you everything he told me. You remember what you and I were doing with those girls behind the bicycle shed at school the other week? Well, Dad wants me to tell you that the birds and the bees do it too.'

A prize bull was on display at an agricultural show. It was kept in a special enclosure and there was a charge of £1 per person to see the mighty beast. A man with twelve children took his whole family along and the ticket attendant said, 'Are all these children yours?'

'They are,' said the man.

'Well, you wait here a minute,' said the attendant, 'and I'll bring the bull out to see you.'

A newly married couple were spending their honeymoon in Rio de Janeiro. One morning, they bought a brightly coloured parrot and took it back to their hotel room. However, the bird kept up a running commentary on their love-making and after a few days of this, the annoyed groom flung a blanket over its cage and shouted, 'If I hear one more word out of you, I'm taking you down to the zoo and leaving you there!'

On the last day of the honeymoon, the couple were packing their clothes away prior to departure. They had bought so many souvenirs that they had great difficulty in closing the last suitcase. They decided that one of them should stand on it while the other attempted to fasten it. 'Darling,' said the groom, 'you get on top and I'll try.' This proved unsuccessful, so the groom said, 'Wait a minute – I'll get on top and you try.' This didn't work either, so the groom said, 'Look, darling, let's both get on top and try.'

At this point, the parrot whipped the blanket off its cage and squawked, 'Zoo or no zoo, this I've got to see!'

Deep in the heart of Morocco, a sheikh decided to set off on a trip across the desert. He was short of a horse, so two of the villagers were ordered to bring their horses to his tent so that he could choose the best one to take. Neither of the villagers wanted to give up his horse and both protested that their steeds were worthless. 'We'll have a race,' said the sheikh. 'I will take the winner.'

'But, sire,' said one of the sheikh's advisers, 'neither man will let his horse go fast.'

'Yes, they will,' replied the sheikh. 'Let each man ride the other's horse.'

A fellow visited Las Vegas and lost all his money at the tables. He didn't even have enough money left to go to the toilet and he was obliged to borrow a coin from another patron of the gaming rooms. When he got to the toilets, however, another fellow was just coming out of one of the cubicles. Holding the door open, this fellow said, 'Here you are – use this one.'

Returning to the tables afterwards, our hero used the coin to play a slot-machine – and won. With his winnings, he went back to the roulette table and by the end of the evening he had won a considerable fortune.

Rich and famous, he went round the country lecturing on his experiences, and declaring that if he ever met his benefactor, he would split his winnings with him. In one audience, a man at the back of the hall jumped up and shouted, 'I'm the man who gave you the coin!'

'You're not the one I'm looking for,' said the lucky winner. 'I'm looking for the man who left the door open!'

A s the bombs fell on London in 1941, the city hospital was being evacuated. Matron was hastily going through her desk drawers. 'Doctor!' she shouted to the Chief Surgeon, 'I can't find my teeth!'

'Never mind about that!' the surgeon shouted back. 'It's bombs they're dropping – not sandwiches!'

A country vicar in a small parish in the West Country had one serious failing – he could never remember names. Whenever he had any announcement to make, he had to write all the names down on a sheet of paper. One morning he delivered a funeral sermon that went something like this: 'Dearly beloved, we are gathered here today to pay tribute to [glancing at his notes] Albert Jones, a man who came here to [glancing at his notes] Shepton Mallett thirty years ago and soon became one of us. He married a local girl [glancing at his notes] Betty Hardcastle, and settled down to raise a family, two fine boys [glancing at his notes], Michael and David. And now at last, after a long and happy life, he rests in the bosom of Our Saviour [glancing at his notes], Jesus Christ!'

A Frenchman came over to London to visit some English friends. He was invited to a neighbour's Silver Wedding Anniversary, a celebration that he knew nothing about. 'What ees this Silvair Wedding?' he asked.

'Well,' said his host, 'it means that Derek and Connie have been living together for twenty-five years.'

'Ah, I see!' said the Frenchman. 'And now they get married! *Formidable!*'

When Pope John Paul II took over the papacy, he caused a certain amount of consternation one Easter. As part of the Easter celebrations, it was the custom for the Chief Rabbi of Rome to enter the Basilica and present the Pope with an ancient scroll. Every year, the Pope would take this scroll, bow to the Rabbi, and hand it back unopened. This ceremony had been going on for centuries and no one could even remember what it signified. The new Pope decided to put an end to this ritual and to the horror of the assembled cardinals, when the scroll was handed to him, he opened it up. It was a bill for the Last Supper.

An old farmer went to his doctor for a medical examination. His doctor had told him to bring a specimen with him, and he handed over a large bottle which was almost full. The doctor examined the sample and then said, 'Excellent – nothing wrong with that at all.'

When he got home some time later, the farmer said to his wife, 'Good news, dear. Neither you nor I, nor the kids, nor grandpa and grandma, nor the horse have a thing the matter with us!'

A fellow was taking a walk in the country when he came upon a large house with a notice by the front door which read: PLEASE RING BELL FOR THE CARETAKER. He rang the bell and an elderly man opened the door. 'Are you the caretaker?' he asked.

'Yes,' said the old man. 'What do you want?'

'I just wondered why you can't ring the bell yourself.'

Calvin Coolidge, President of the United States (1923–1929), was noted for being a man of very few words. At a White House press conference, one of the reporters asked him whether he had any comments to make about Prohibition. 'No,' replied Coolidge.

'Have you anything to say about the agricultural situation?' asked another reporter.

'No,' said Coolidge.

'What about the forthcoming senatorial campaign – have you anything to say about that?' asked another press man.

'No,' said Coolidge. As the reporters began to file out of the room, he called after them, 'And don't quote me.'

There was once a fellow who was sent for psychiatric treatment because he was suffering from delusions. He was firmly convinced that he would shortly receive a letter that would make him rich. The letter would be from a firm of solicitors telling him that a distant relative had died and left him a vast estate in Scotland and a priceless collection of art and antiques. The psychiatrist worked very hard over a period of months to cure him of this delusion. And just when he had the man cured, the letter arrived.

A survey on sexual habits was being carried out by a popular newspaper and one questioner stopped an elderly Italian gentleman in the street who was wearing a black suit and asked him how often he had sexual intercourse. 'Oh, about half a dozen times a year,' said the gentleman. The questioner smiled.

'I thought you Italians were supposed to be sexy,' she said.

'We are,' said the gentleman. 'But I don't think half a dozen times a year is so bad for a seventy-two-year-old priest with no car.'

'Well, Jimmy,' said the proud father, 'how did your first riding lesson go?'

'Great, Dad,' said Jimmy. 'I made friends with the horse and I even gave him a drink of water.' Dad smiled.

'I think you're supposed to say you watered the horse,' he said.

'Am I?' said Jimmy. 'All right. I watered the horse. And now I'm going to milk the cat.'

Suzanne the maid was leaving to get married. 'I'm very pleased for you, Suzanne,' said her mistress. 'You will have it much easier now that you're getting married.'

'Yes, madam,' said Suzanne. 'And more frequently I hope.'

Mark Twain used to receive a large number of photographs from men who thought they looked like him. Twain got fed up with answering these letters so he had a form letter printed which read:

DEAR SIR,
Thank you very much for your letter and photograph. In my opinion you are more like me than any other of my numerous doubles. I may even say that you resemble me more closely than I do myself. In fact, I intend to use your picture to shave by.

A farmer's wife went to the chemist to pick up two bottles of medicine. 'Now you be sure to label those bottles

clearly,' she said. 'I must know which one is for the horse and which one is for my husband. I don't want nothing to happen to that horse before we get the spring ploughing done!'

There was a report in the newspapers recently about a man who got married so many times, he married one of his ex-wives without realizing it. He never would have known but for the fact that he recognized his mother-in-law.

At a recent lecture on sexual habits, the lecturer said that sex could be regarded as a form of communication. A member of the audience stood up and asked, 'Does that mean that masturbation is sort of like talking to yourself?'

The office manager was completely bald. Naturally, he was continually being teased by the other members of the staff and he was becoming increasingly irritated. One morning, a brash young executive ran his hand across the manager's bald pate and said, 'Do you know, this feels just like my wife's bottom!'

The manager ran his own hand across his bald scalp and said, 'You're right. It does!'

A Balkan peasant was riding through the forest one sunny morning in the early years of this century. He pulled his horse up just in time to avoid treading on a frog. But this was no ordinary frog. This was a magic frog, and as a reward for saving its life, it granted the peasant three wishes. The peasant said that he would like to be extremely rich, of royal birth, and married to a beautiful young girl.

There was a blinding flash, a puff of smoke, and the peasant found himself lying in a magnificent four-poster bed, under a royal coat-of-arms. Beside him was a beautiful young girl in a silken nightdress. 'Hurry up, Franz Ferdinand,' she said. 'We're due in Sarajevo in half an hour.'

A door-to-door salesman specializing in toilet articles arrived at a remote cottage in the country. He tried in vain to make a sale but the woman at the door was obviously reluctant to spend any money. Finally the salesman said, 'Well, how about this – it's our latest line – a lavatory brush. Excellent quality.' This seemed to interest the woman and, to the salesman's delight, she bought one.

A few months later, he was passing the same cottage and he knocked on the door and asked the woman whether she had found the lavatory brush satisfactory. 'Oh, yes,' she said. 'I like it very much. But my husband's a bit old-fashioned, you know. He still prefers toilet paper.'

A small boy was taken to see an exhibition of abstract art at the Tate Gallery. His mother pointed to one painting and said, 'That is supposed to be a man on a horse.'

And the little boy said, 'Well, why isn't it?'

A fellow went in to see a psychiatrist and the doctor said, 'What seems to be the problem?'

'Oh, there's nothing wrong with me,' said the man. 'I'm Napoleon. It's my wife, Josephine. She thinks she's Mrs Brown.'

One Saturday afternoon, there was a commotion on the golf course as a young lady dressed in a resplendent wedding-gown stormed on to the green, strode over to a young golfer, and screamed, 'You miserable, no-good bastard! Do you know what time it is?'

The young golfer looked up from his putt and said, 'But Sylvia, I told you – only if it was raining!'

At a recent school nativity play near London, three six-year-olds were playing the part of the kings. During the scene in the stable, the first stepped forward with his gift and said, 'Gold.' The second stepped forward and said, 'Myrrh.' Then the third stepped forward and said, 'And Frank sent this.'

Two schoolboys at Eton became bitter enemies. When they left school, one went into the Church and the other into the Navy. The years passed and the first boy became a bishop, while the second attained the rank of admiral.

One day, the bishop, now grown fat, was standing on platform seven at Paddington station when he caught sight of his old enemy, resplendent in full admiral's uniform. 'I say, porter,' he said with a sly smile, 'is this the right platform for Oxford?'

'It is, madam,' said the admiral without batting an eye, 'but do you think you should be travelling in your condition?'

On a long-distance British Airways flight to Australia, a mother took her young son to the toilet and told him she would come back for him in five minutes. However, he was finished in two minutes so he left the toilet and wandered off down the aisle in the opposite direction to where his mother was sitting so she didn't notice.

Meanwhile, a businessman entered the toilet and locked the door. After the five minutes were up, the mother went to the toilet, knocked on the door and called out, 'Do you need any help with your zipper?'

From behind the door, a startled male voice said, 'Good God, that's what I call service!'

A well-known actor landed the lead in a smash hit West End musical. With the prospect of a long run at a fabulous salary, he decided to have his apartment redecorated from top to bottom, and engaged a painter and decorator for the job. In order to get off on the right foot, he presented the decorator with a couple of expensive front-row tickets for the show.

At the end of the first month he received a bill from the decorator, for the first four weeks' work. One of the items read: *4 hours overtime watching customer sing and dance.*

Two Frenchmen were arguing over the precise meaning of the word 'savoir-faire'. Pierre said, 'If you're making love to another man's wife and the husband bursts in and catches you at it and says, "Go ahead", that's "savoir-faire".'

'No, no,' said Jean-Paul. 'If the husband bursts in and says "Go ahead", and you *do* go ahead — *that's* "savoir-faire"!'

A salesman walked up to a house one morning and saw a little boy playing on the front step. 'Hello, sonny,' he said. 'Is your mother in?'

'Yes,' said the little lad, so the salesman knocked on the door. There was no reply, so he knocked again and waited patiently. No one answered his knock, so he turned to the little boy and said, 'I thought you said your mother was in?'

'She is,' said the lad. 'But we don't live here.'

A young fellow laboured under the delusion that he was a Yorkshire terrier. His friends persuaded him to seek professional help and he went to a psychiatrist for a course of treatment. Some weeks later, he met one of his friends in the street. 'And how are things now?' asked his friend. 'Did the psychiatrist cure you?'

'Oh, yes,' said the young fellow. 'I'm quite OK now. Fit as a fiddle — here, feel my nose.'

The vicar glanced out of his study window and saw Mrs Robinson coming up the garden path. Now Mrs Robinson was a terrible bore, so he rushed upstairs to his

bedroom and left his wife to entertain the unwelcome guest.

Half an hour later, he tiptoed out on to the landing and hearing no sound from the living-room, he called down, 'Has that horrible old bore gone yet, dear?'

With admirable presence of mind, his wife called back, 'Yes, dear, she went ages ago. Mrs Robinson is here now.'

A young married couple decided they needed an au pair and arranged for a girl to come over from northern Finland. When she arrived, the wife asked, 'Can you cook?'

'No,' said the Finnish girl. 'My mother always did the cooking.'

'Can you do the housework?' asked the wife.

'No,' said the girl. 'My older sister always did the housework.'

'Well, then,' said the wife, 'you'd better just look after the children.'

'I don't know how to do that,' said the girl. 'My younger sister always took care of the children in our family.'

The wife looked at her husband in despair. 'What can you do then?' she asked.

'Well,' said the Finnish girl brightly, 'I can milk reindeer.'

A fellow tried to get on a British Airways flight with a little Yorkshire terrier in his arms. The stewardess told him that dogs were not allowed on board so he went to the airport shop and bought himself a pair of dark glasses and a white walking-stick. This time he was greeted by another stewardess who said, 'It's quite unusual to see a Yorkshire terrier as a guide dog, sir. They're usually Golden Labradors.'

'You mean this isn't a Golden Labrador!' said the man in surprise.

A blind golfer once challenged a well-known professional to a game. 'But that would be taking an unfair advantage of you,' protested the pro.

'Not at all,' said the blind man. 'And furthermore, I'll play you for £50 a hole.'

'Well, if you insist,' said the pro. 'When would you like to play?'

'Any night,' said the blind man. 'Any night at all.'

The Queen was visiting a remote Scottish town when she was introduced to a man, his wife and his twelve children. 'Are all of these your children?' she asked, and the man said, 'Yes, they are, Your Majesty.'

'Good gracious!' said the Queen. 'We ought to give you a knighthood!'

'He's got one,' said the wife. 'But he refuses to wear it!'

Two African big game hunters were having lunch in their club. They became engaged in a heated argument and one of them said, 'I'm absolutely certain, old boy, that the word is spelled "w-h-o-o-m-b".'

'Nonsense, old chap,' protested the other. 'It's spelled "w-o-o-m".'

A waitress who just happened to be passing said, 'Excuse

me, gentlemen, I couldn't help overhearing. I think the word is spelled "w-o-m-b".'

One of the hunters turned to the other and said, 'It's obvious, old boy, that this young lady has never heard a bull elephant fart.'

A young lady had just emerged from a hot bath when the doorbell rang. Dripping wet, she ran to the door and called out, 'I can't let you in – I've just got out of the bath.'

'That's all right, lady,' said a voice from the other side of the door. 'I'm a blind salesman.'

'All right, then,' said the young lady and she opened the door.

'Thanks,' said the man. 'Where shall I put the blinds?'

A fellow visiting a small town in a remote area of Ireland wandered into the local snooker hall one evening in search of a game. He was shown to the only table in the place, which was very much the worse for wear. Not only that, there was only one broken-down old cue, and the balls were all of the same, dirty-grey colour. 'I can't play with these!' he protested. 'How am I supposed to tell the reds from the white?'

'It's OK, sir,' said the manager. 'You'll get to know them by their shape.'

Hearing that London Zoo was in danger of closing down, an Irish visitor to London decided to pay a visit. He stopped in front of the kangaroo cage and appeared to be fascinated by the animals. 'Do you have a special interest in these?' asked a passing attendant.

'I do that,' said the Irishman and pointed to a notice on the cage which read: A NATIVE OF AUSTRALIA. 'My sister married one!'

A well-known explorer set off for an expedition in New Guinea and was captured by a tribe of head-hunters. After some weeks he managed to escape and he immediately telephoned his wife to say he was safe. 'I need some clothes, dear,' he said. 'Will you send out a bush jacket, size 40 short, some tropical shirts, 16 collar, and a pair of strong shoes, size 8. Oh, and I need a hat.'

'What size hat?' his wife asked.

'One and seven-eighths.'

A young lady was talking to an astronomer at a party. 'I can understand how you people work out how far the stars are from the earth, and what their sizes are,' she said, 'but how on earth do you find out what their names are?'

At the start of the Irish racing season, a horsebox arrived at one of the courses, and when the stable lads opened the doors, they found that the box was empty. 'Well,' said the driver in explanation, 'somebody has to bring the non-runners!'

A soldier serving overseas received a photograph from his girlfriend which showed two couples arm in arm while she sat alone to one side. In the accompanying letter she explained that she was being very good and saving herself only for him. Delighted, he showed the photograph and the letter to a friend. His pal studied them carefully and then said, 'Yes, but who took the picture?'

An MP was visiting Moscow on a fact-finding tour and he discovered that he was expected to make a speech. He decided to deliver his address in Russian so he had a Russian-speaking member of the British Embassy draw up a short speech and then learned it phonetically. On his way to deliver his address, he remembered that he had forgotten to find out the Russian for 'Ladies and Gentlemen' as his introduction. Just then, he passed a public convenience so he stopped the car and made a note of the Russian words over the entrance.

At the dinner, he rose to give his address and was very surprised that his opening words were greeted with gales of laughter. The rest of his speech went quite well, and afterwards, he asked his friend at the British Embassy, who had also been present, why everyone had laughed so much when he started speaking. 'Well,' said his friend, 'it might have been that you started off with "Male and female urinals".'

A Londoner decided to try a pony-trekking holiday for a change, though he had never ridden in his life and knew nothing about ponies or horses. As he was preparing to set off in the stable yard on the first morning, the instructor said, 'Excuse me – you're putting the saddle on backwards.'

'Oh yeah?' said the novice. 'And 'ow do you know which way I'm going to go?'

It was the first day at the new school and the children had been instructed to bring in their birth certificates for the school records. Four-year-old Janet came home that afternoon in tears. 'What's the matter, dear?' her mother asked.

And little Janet sobbed, 'I've lost my excuse for being born!'

Two married couples went away on holiday together to Spain. At the end of the first week, they were bored to tears, and one of the husbands suggested that they swap partners to try and liven things up a bit. They all agreed it was worth a try. The following morning, the husband who had suggested the exchange said, 'I'm glad we tried this. It was fun. Let's go and see how the girls got on.'

An explorer was walking through the jungle when he came across a poisonous snake. He walked cautiously round it and then he noticed that it wasn't a snake at all but a stick. 'I was absolutely terrified,' he told a friend that evening.

'But if it was only a stick,' said his friend, 'why were you terrified?'

'Because,' said the explorer, 'the stick I picked up to hit it with *was* a snake!'

Bill had been married for fifteen years and one night he took a friend home to dinner. As they entered the house, Bill's wife came running up to him, threw her arms round his neck, and kissed him affectionately.

'You're a lucky guy, Bill,' said his friend. 'Married for fifteen years and you still get a welcome like that when you come home.'

'It doesn't mean a thing,' said Bill. 'She only does it to make the dog jealous.'

The Archbishop of Canterbury was making his first visit to New York. His advisers suggested that he should be very diplomatic and tactful in answering questions from press and TV reporters, so as to avoid any controversy. There was a huge crowd of reporters waiting to greet him and, as he stepped from the plane, one of them thrust a microphone in his face and said, 'Say, Bishop, what's your opinion of the large number of brothels in Manhattan?'

Remembering that he had to be tactful, and suffering slightly from jet-lag, the Archbishop said cautiously, 'Are there any brothels in Manhattan?'

The following morning, the headlines of the New York Times read: ARCHBISHOP'S FIRST QUESTION ON ARRIVING IN NEW YORK – 'ARE THERE ANY BROTHELS IN MANHATTAN?'

The mother of a teenage boy was asked by his headmaster to call in at his office to discuss a serious matter. When she arrived, the headmaster said, 'I'm sorry to have to tell you that your son came to school yesterday wearing a print dress, high-heeled court shoes and lipstick!'

'Damn it!' said the boy's mother. 'I've told him a hundred times not to wear his father's clothes!'

Two photography enthusiasts were discussing their day at a bar in Barcelona. 'I saw an old beggar this morning,' said one, 'down on the Ramblas. He was wearing filthy rags, and he looked really ill and desperate.'

'Poor chap,' sympathized his pal. 'What did you give him?'

'Well, the light was pretty good so I gave him f-16 at 1/100.'

The year was 1916. Captain Fotheringham of the Royal Flying Corps had just shot down the German air ace Baron von Hohingen over the English lines. The Baron had survived the crash and Captain Fotheringham went to visit him in hospital. 'Is there anything I can do for you, old boy?' he asked.

'Yes, there is,' said the Baron. 'They are going to amputate my left leg. Would you drop it over Germany for me?'

'Leave it to me, old bean,' said Captain Fotheringham, and that very day he carried out the request.

A week later, he returned to the hospital for another visit and this time the German said, 'May I ask you another favour? They are going to remove my right leg. Once again, would you drop it over the Fatherland?'

So once again, Fotheringham carried out the strange request, and the following day he paid a further visit to the hospital. 'Captain,' said von Hohingen, 'this afternoon, they are going to remove my right arm. Once again, could I ask you to drop it behind the German lines?'

'Of course, old chap,' said Captain Fotheringham thoughtfully. 'But I say, look here, you're not trying to escape, are you?'

'I've got an infallible betting system for the races,' said Smithers. 'I just think of something that has happened to me recently, and then I look for a horse that fits. I'll give you an example. A couple of weeks ago, I dropped the teapot – so I backed "Broken China" and it romped home at twenty to one. Then the day after I had been playing roulette at the casino, I backed "Wheel of Fortune" – it won. Last Christmas, we went to the pantomime, so I backed "Cinderella" at a hundred to eight and it came in second – I cleared £250.'

'Sounds good to me,' said Brown. 'I'll try it.'

When they met in the pub a week later, Smithers said, 'How did you get on with my betting system?'

'Didn't work for me,' said Brown. 'I was walking to work yesterday and my hat blew off. The nearest horse I could find was "Winds of Change".'

'And did it win?' asked Smithers.

'Came in last,' said Brown. 'The winner was some French horse called "Mon Chapeau".'

In an effort to boost sales, British Airways announced that for two weeks only, any business executive who travelled on a midweek flight could take his wife along with him for only twenty per cent of the normal fare. In order to judge the success of this experiment, they wrote to all the wives concerned, asking them if they had enjoyed their flights. Eighty-five per cent of the wives wrote back asking, 'What flight?'

An American visiting England started to chat up a pretty young thing in a bar. 'You know,' he said conversationally, 'I come from the other side.'

'Let's go home at once,' said the girl, finishing her drink quickly. 'This I've got to see!'

'I had a funny old dream last night,' a chap in the local said to his pal. 'I dreamed I went to Dreamland at Margate and had a wonderful time on the roller coaster.'

'I had a dream last night too,' said his friend. 'I dreamed I was alone in my room with Madonna! And then the door opened and in walked Michelle Pfeiffer and Julia Roberts!'

'Well, you're a fine one,' said the first fellow. 'Why didn't you telephone me?'

'I did,' said his pal. 'But your wife told me you'd gone to Margate.'

One afternoon, the telephone rang in the doctor's surgery. It was the young lady he had been examining that morning. 'Would you mind having a look round your office, doctor?' she said. 'I think I left my panties there.'

The doctor had a good look round his office and then said, 'I'm sorry but they don't seem to be here.'

'Oh, well,' said the young lady, 'never mind. I suppose I must have left them at the dentist's.'

A trombone player was rehearsing late at night in his room when there was a knock on the door. He opened it to find an irate neighbour who said, 'Hey! Do you know there's a little old lady sick next door?'

'No,' said the musician. 'But if you hum a few bars, I'll improvise.'

The boss was extremely annoyed when his secretary made a couple of corrections in a letter he had dictated. 'You're not paid to correct my work,' he stormed. 'Just type it out exactly as I dictated it — no corrections, no additions, no deletions.'

The next letter that his secretary produced for signature read as follows:

DEAR MR DEAN
— I don't know whether the idiot spells it with an e on the end — you can look it up — in reply to your letter of the — where the hell's that letter — oh, well, look it up yourself — the price you quote is far too high — greedy old sod! — and we would suggest a figure nearer to our initial estimate — estimate, huh! — blind guess would be nearer the mark — we await your comments — and if you don't like it you can lump it! — usual bumph at the end — and isn't it about time for a coffee?

On the day before the Battle of Hastings, King Harold said to his commander of the army, 'Are the troops all ready?'

'They are, Your Majesty,' said the commander. 'Would you like a demonstration?'

'Yes, I would,' said the king. So the commander lined all the archers up and instructed them to fire off a volley. Three thousand arrows sped through the air and landed a quarter of a mile away. But one clumsy archer fired straight up into the air, and the arrow went up several hundred feet, turned round and came back down again, landing about six inches from where the king was standing.

'You want to watch that fellow,' said the king. 'If he's not careful, he'll have somebody's eye out tomorrow!'

A French diplomat was on a visit to London, and his host, an MP, took him round all the sights and gave him a good time. On the last day of his visit, the Frenchman was asked if he would like to pay a visit to the House of Commons. 'It is very kind of you,' he said, 'but I must not cockroach on your time any further.'

'That's all right,' said the MP. 'But I hope you won't mind my pointing it out – the word is "encroach" not "cockroach".'

'Ah, I see,' replied the Frenchman. 'It is a question of gender!'

The famous millionaire John D. Rockefeller had a very strict upbringing. Discipline in the Rockefeller household was severe in the extreme. On one occasion, he was receiving a caning from his mother, during the course of which he managed to convince her that he was not guilty of the offence for which he was being punished.

'Very well,' said his mother. 'But we have gone so far that we may as well proceed. It will be credited to your account for next time.'

A missionary in Africa came upon a witch doctor pounding away at a large drum. 'What are you doing?' asked the missionary.

'We have no water,' said the witch doctor.

'I see,' said the missionary. 'So I suppose you're praying for rain?'

'No,' said the witch doctor. 'I'm calling the plumber.'

A man was walking along the banks of a canal when he noticed a chap struggling in the water. 'What's your name?' he shouted.

'Alf Brown,' the man in the water shouted back. 'But get me out of here – I'm drowning!'

'Where do you work?' shouted the man on the bank.

'At the coal mine down the road!'

The fellow on the bank immediately walked off and presented himself to the manager of the coal mine. 'Do you have an Alf Brown working here?' he asked.

'We do,' said the manager.

'Well, I've come for his job – he's just drowned in the canal.'

'You're too late,' said the manager. 'The fellow that pushed him in has got it.'

'How old are you, Grandma?' asked little Samantha. 'Oh, I don't know, dear,' said Grandma with a smile. 'I've had so many birthdays, I've lost count!'

'Well, why don't you look in your knickers,' said Samantha. 'Mine say three to four years old.'

A well-known duke used to take breakfast in bed at his country estate and one morning a new maid came in with the breakfast tray. She was very young and pretty and the duke said, 'Good morning, my dear. You're new, aren't you?'

'Yes, sir,' said the maid as she put down the tray.

'You're a pretty little thing,' said the duke. 'Come and sit here on the bed.'

'Yes, sir,' said the girl and she sat down on the bed.

'You must learn the correct way to address me,' said the duke. 'Now, first of all, you must say "Your Grace".'

So the girl got down on her knees at the side of the bed and said, 'For what I am about to receive, may the Lord make me truly thankful.'

An angler returned from a day on the river, carrying the biggest fish the club had ever seen. It was fully three feet long and was obviously a record-breaker. His bitterest rival in the angling club came in shortly afterwards carrying three or four tiny fishes on a string. The first fisherman smiled and pointed silently at his monster catch. The second angler looked at it for a few moments and then said, 'Just caught the one, I see.'

A couple of American golfing enthusiasts came over on a visit and went up to St Andrews for a game. 'What's the course fee?' they asked the secretary.

'As you're American visitors,' he said, 'there'll be no charge.'

'Gee, that's swell,' said the Americans. 'Could we hire some clubs?'

'Certainly,' said the secretary. 'Help yourself – there'll be nothing to pay.'

Delighted, the Americans said, 'And could we have some balls?'

'Of course,' said the secretary, handing over a set. 'That'll be £150.'

The Americans paid up and as they walked off to the first tee, one of them said, 'These Limeys! When they grab you, they certainly know where to do it!'

A strong supporter of the Women's Liberation movement was holding a committee meeting in her house. 'We have some guests with us tonight,' she said. 'I'd like you all to welcome Mr and Mrs Forbes-Robertson.' Then, remembering where she was, she added, 'Not necessarily in that order, of course!'

A little girl wandered into the bathroom whilst her mother was taking a bath and said, 'Mummy – why is your tummy so big?'

'Well, you see,' said her mother, 'Daddy has given me a baby.'

Downstairs later on, the little girl said to her father, 'Daddy, did you give Mummy a little baby?'

'Yes, I did,' said Daddy, smiling.

'Well,' said the little girl, 'I think she's eaten it!'

A travelling salesman found himself stranded in a small village one winter's night. He knocked on the door of a farmhouse and asked the farmer if he would put him up for the night. 'All right,' said the farmer, 'as long as you don't mind sharing a room with my young son.'

'My God!' said the salesman. 'I'm in the wrong joke!'

The orchestra had just finished playing Tchaikovsky's *Nutcracker Suite*. A lady in the third row of the stalls turned to her husband and said, 'I do hope they're going to play Tchaikovsky's *Nutcracker Suite*.'

'They've just finished playing it!' said her husband.

'Well, you might have told me!' said the matron. 'It's my favourite piece!'

A fellow who had great difficulty getting to sleep at night went to see his doctor. The doctor prescribed some sleeping pills and that night he took a pill and fell asleep as soon as his head touched the pillow. He woke feeling completely refreshed, bright and alive, and went off to work with a spring in his step.

Walking into the office he said to his boss, 'You'll be glad to know I had no trouble getting to sleep last night and I woke up this morning even before the alarm went off.'

'That's great,' said his boss. 'But where were you yesterday?'

A representative for a publishing firm plodded round his territory for months without making a single sale. He began to grow desperate. He couldn't keep up his mortgage payments, his wife had to take a job, and the bills were mounting up. Finally, after eight months, he made his first sale – and then realized that he'd forgotten the name of the firm he was working for.

A maid had been employed by the same family for several years. One day she told her mistress that she would have to leave because she was pregnant. 'Well,' said her mistress, 'as you have no husband, and rather than lose you, we'll adopt the child.'

A year later, the maid again found herself pregnant, and once again, her mistress agreed to adopt the baby rather than lose her services.

Twelve months later, the maid was pregnant again, and once more her mistress offered to adopt the child. 'No, I'm definitely leaving this time,' said the maid. 'I couldn't work for a family that has three children.'

A fellow was waiting in a doctor's reception when a young girl came out of the surgery sobbing bitterly. 'What's the matter?' he asked sympathetically.

'The doctor's just told me I'm pregnant,' she said.

It was the fellow's turn next and when he went into the doctor's surgery, he said, 'Is that young lady really pregnant?'

'No,' said the doctor, 'but it's cured her hiccups.'

A confirmed atheist was visiting the house of a vicar. He noticed a very beautiful gold and silver model of the solar system with a globe representing the earth, surrounded by all the planets. 'I'd love one of those,' said the atheist. 'Who made it?'

'Oh, nobody made it,' said the vicar. 'It just happened.'

A chap was driving through Ireland on holiday when he came across a pile of stones with a red light on top of it in the middle of the road. He pulled up just in time and asked a farmer who was leaning over a nearby gate what the light was for. 'It's to keep motorists from running into the pile of stones, of course,' said the farmer.

'But what are the stones for?' asked the motorist.

'Why, to put the light on,' said the farmer.

A man on holiday in Las Vegas lost all his money at the tables. He went up to a rich Texan at the bar and said, 'Would you lend me $100 – I think my luck's turning and I'll be able to pay you back in no time.' The Texan generously lent him $100 and the fellow went back to the roulette wheel where he lost the lot in five minutes.

The next evening, he again managed to borrow $100 from the rich Texan, and once again he lost it all at the roulette wheel. This continued every night for a week. And then, one evening in the bar, the unlucky punter told his best friend all about it and asked him what he'd advise. 'There's only one thing you can do,' said his friend. 'Stay away from the bum! He's bad luck for you!'

An angler was regaling his friends with tales of the day's fishing. 'I ran short of bait this morning,' he said, 'but when I glanced down, I noticed a small snake with a frog in its mouth. I removed the frog and cut it up for bait. Feeling sorry for depriving the snake of its lunch, I took out my hip flask and gave it a nip of whisky. The snake glided off and I went back to my rod. About half an hour later, I felt something against my boot. I looked down — and there was the same snake with three more frogs.'

A fellow applied for a job and the personnel manager said, 'I'm sorry but I can't help you. What with the recession, we're over-staffed as it is — there just isn't enough work to go round.'

'That's all right,' said the applicant. 'The little bit of work I would do wouldn't be noticed.'

An insurance salesman was trying to sell a policy to a factory owner. 'I've got all the insurance I need,' said the executive. 'Fire, accident, employer's liability, the lot, so don't waste your time.'

'Are you covered against floods?' asked the salesman.

'Floods?' said the businessman with interest. 'How do you arrange a flood?'

A so-called New Evangelist was travelling round the country preaching the gospel. He put up for the night at a small hotel and after he had got settled into his room, he

called down to the pretty blonde receptionist and asked her to come up to his room, as soon as she finished work. Out of curiosity she did so and was amazed, when she entered his room at about 11 o'clock, to find him undressed and in bed. 'Get in, my dear,' he said, holding back the bedclothes for her.

'But I thought you were a man of God!' she said, slightly bewildered.

'It's quite all right, my dear,' said the preacher. 'There's nothing wrong in it – it's written in the Bible.'

Somewhat reassured, she undressed and got into bed and they made love several times through the night. Every time she expressed doubts about what they were doing, the preacher calmed her fears by saying, 'It's written in the Bible.'

The next day, after he had left, she went up to his room to try to find out exactly where it was 'written in the Bible'. Opening the Gideon Bible on the bedside table, she saw inscribed on the flyleaf the words: 'The blonde receptionist is a very good screw.'

There had been severe flooding throughout the West Country and the vicar was stranded on the roof of the church. A rowing boat passed close by and one of the rowers shouted, 'Come on down, vicar – get in the boat!'

'Save the others!' the vicar shouted. 'The Lord will save me!'

The waters continued to rise and just as they reached the vicar's waist, a motor boat chugged up. Again the vicar cried, 'Save the others! The Lord will save me!'

The motor boat chugged off and an hour passed. By the time the helicopter arrived, the water was up to the vicar's chin. 'Hang on!' shouted the helicopter pilot. 'We'll lower a rope!'

'No, no!' shouted the vicar. 'The Lord will save me!'

As the helicopter flew off, the waters rose still further and the vicar disappeared from view. When he arrived in Heaven, he said indignantly to God, 'Oh Lord – why did you let me down? I was sure you would save me!'

'What do you mean – let you down?' said God. 'I sent two boats and a helicopter to take you off that roof, didn't I?'

The world's most brilliant salesman once managed to sell a refrigerator to an Eskimo. Some months later, he called round again to see how the Eskimo was getting on with his new purchase. 'OK,' said the Eskimo, 'but I haven't quite got the knack of chopping up the ice into little squares to fit the tray.'

A young lady was regaling her friends with intimate details about her honeymoon. 'As soon as we got to the hotel,' she said, 'Roger rushed me up to the room, undressed us both, and we had a performance. Then just before dinner we had another performance. After dinner, we went upstairs and had another performance. During the night he woke me up three times and we had a performance each time. Then just before breakfast we had a dress rehearsal.'

'What's a dress rehearsal?' asked one of her friends.

'It's the same as a performance,' said the young lady, 'but nobody comes.'

Some time towards the end of the eighteenth century, an Englishman and an Italian quarrelled. Neither of them wanted to fight a duel, but their friend persuaded them that this was the only right thing to do. It was agreed that they would fight with pistols, alone in a darkened room. The candles were put out, and the Englishman, not wishing to harm the Italian, fired up the chimney – and hit the Italian in the backside.

During a heavy raid on London at the height of the Blitz, an air-raid warden shouted down from the entrance to a shelter, 'Are there any expectant mothers down there?'

'It's hard to say,' shouted a female voice. 'We've only been down here ten minutes!'

A woman walked into a psychiatrist's office carrying a duck under her arm. 'What seems to be the problem?' asked the psychiatrist.

'Well, it's not me, actually,' said the woman. 'It's my husband. He thinks he's a duck.'

'I understand you're a doctor,' said a lady at a cocktail party. 'I wonder if I could ask you a question? I've been getting these pains in my side and sometimes in my leg as well.'

'I'm sorry,' the man interrupted, 'I'm not that kind of doctor. I'm a Doctor of Economics.'

'Oh, I see,' said the lady. 'Well, in that case, should I sell my British Telecom shares?'

Moskowitz rang Goldstein to ask how business was going. 'Fine, fine,' said Goldstein. 'Even with the recession, sales are up fifteen per cent. I'm thinking of expanding into the overseas market. On top of that, my son, the doctor, has opened his own private practice and is making £200,000 a year. And my daughter, the lawyer, has been made a senior partner in the firm, and has just won a big civil case with a fee of £50,000 . . .'

'I'll phone back later,' interrupted Moskowitz. 'I didn't realize you had someone with you.'

'And does anyone know where God lives?' asked the Sunday School teacher.

'In our bathroom,' said a little boy in the front row.

'What on earth makes you say that?' asked the teacher.

'Well,' replied the lad, 'every morning my Dad thumps on the door and shouts, "God, are you still in there!" '

The new member of the exclusive golf club was behaving very badly at dinner. He was obviously very drunk and cursed and swore continuously at the waiters. A senior committee member approached him and said, 'Look here, I am the Chairman of the Greens Committee . . .'

'Just the chap I want to see!' said the new member. 'These bloody sprouts are cold!'

The old man was dying and he called his wife and family to his bedside. There were four sons – three fine, big boys and a little one. He said to his wife in a weak voice, 'Don't lie to me now – I want to know the truth. The little one – is he really mine?'

'Oh, yes, dear,' said his wife. 'He really is – I give you my word of honour.'

The old man smiled and slipped peacefully away. With a sigh of relief, the widow muttered, 'Thank God he didn't ask me about the other three!'

A young English couple emigrated to America and went house-hunting in Alabama where they had decided to settle. The real estate agent showed them one house which appeared to be perfect and they clinched the deal there and then. When they got back to their hotel, they realized that they hadn't seen a WC in the house so they wrote to the agent and asked where the WC was located. Now of course in America, the term 'WC' is not used. The agent puzzled for a while and then came to the conclusion that they must mean 'Wesleyan Chapel'.

So he wrote back as follows: 'The WC is located about ten miles from the house. I realize this is rather a long way away, especially if you're in the habit of going regularly. However, it's well worth a visit – some folks take a picnic lunch and make a day of it. It's a fine old building and seats two hundred people. Next year, they're thinking of holding a raffle to raise funds to instal plush seats. I often wish I could go more often myself, but perhaps we'll meet up there some time.'

Two business executives were dining in an expensive restaurant. One of them called the waiter over and said, 'Could you lend us a 10p piece — we want to settle a bet.' The waiter handed over the coin, which was duly flipped, and the bet settled. When the waiter brought the bill, the final item read: *Loan of 10p piece — £1.50.*

Father was reading the paper one evening when his small son came in and said, 'Daddy, will you take me to the zoo tomorrow?'

'No,' his father answered. 'If the zoo wants you, let them come and get you.'

An American soldier in wartime London was telling the customers in a bar about his impressions of England. 'This country's wide open!' he enthused. 'A guy can get anything he wants for a pack of cigarettes and some gum!'

Two rather refined English brothers were listening. One of them was rather deaf and he turned to the other and asked, 'What's he saying?'

'He says he likes England,' said the other.

'And those English broads!' the American continued. 'They're game for anything! Just give them the nod and they're away!'

'What's he saying?' said the deaf brother.

'He says he likes English women,' said the other.

'Take last night,' continued the American. 'I met up with this rich old broad, and before I knew it, I was back in her apartment! She sank a bottle of Scotch in no time flat — then she ripped off her clothes, dragged me into the bedroom, and we were at it all night!'

'What's he saying?' asked the deaf brother.

And the other brother replied, 'He says he's met Mother.'

There are two gates into Heaven. One has a sign saying: QUEUE HERE ALL MEN WHO ARE *NOT* HENPECKED BY THEIR WIVES. The other gate has a sign saying: QUEUE HERE ALL MEN WHO *ARE* HENPECKED BY THEIR WIVES.

Reporting for duty one morning, St Peter saw a long line of men queuing up by the second gate, and one small, meek-looking man standing by the first gate. He asked the little man what his qualifications were for standing by the gate with the sign saying: QUEUE HERE ALL MEN WHO ARE *NOT* HENPECKED BY THEIR WIVES.

'I don't know really,' said the man. 'My wife told me to come and queue here.'

A very rich lady visited her favourite designer and said, 'I need a new hat – something glamorous and startling, yet simple in design.' Jean-Paul pulled out a length of beautiful ribbon and began to cut and fold it. In five minutes he had produced a beautiful and original hat.

'That will be £500, madame,' he said.

'£500!' said the lady. 'That's an outrageous price for a simple length of ribbon!'

Without a word, Jean-Paul unwound the ribbon and dismantled the hat. Handing the ribbon to the lady, he said quietly, 'The ribbon itself, madame, is yours for nothing.'

A young business executive from Hong Kong came over to England for a holiday. He met an attractive young lady and invited her to come back with him to Hong Kong – as his wife, of course – all fair and above board. She willingly agreed, and after the wedding in London, they flew back to the Far East.

On the first morning after their return, the husband had to leave early for the office, so he got out of bed quietly and left without waking his wife. A few minutes later, the Chinese servant came into the bedroom and shook the young bride's shoulder. 'Come along, missy,' he said. 'Time to get dressed and go home!'

A young Spanish girl married the handsomest man in the village and on their wedding night she was pleasantly surprised by his vigour and manhood. 'Oh, Miguel,' she cried. 'You are so magnificently endowed!'

'Yes,' said Miguel proudly, 'and I alone in the whole village have such prodigious equipment!'

After a few weeks, Miguel had to go away for a couple of weeks for the sheep-shearing. When he returned, his bride met him at the door and said angrily, 'Miguel, you lied to me! You said you alone in the whole village were so magnificently endowed but it is not true! Don Antonio also has one just as good as yours!'

Miguel thought quickly. 'Ah, I forgot to tell you!' he said. 'You see, I had two – and I gave one to my friend, Don Antonio.'

'You fool!' screamed his wife. 'You gave him the best one!'

A rabbi, a Protestant minister, a Catholic priest and a Baptist preacher were discussing religion. The rabbi said, 'Let's be honest with each other. We all have our vices. For instance, I'm not supposed to eat ham or pork – but I love them!'

The Protestant minister said, 'Well, I do have one vice – I like my drink. In fact, I get really pissed from time to time.'

The Catholic priest said, 'I'll be honest. I like girls. I like to get laid at least once a week.'

They looked at the Baptist preacher. 'Haven't you got any vices?' they asked.

'Well, only one,' he said. 'I like to gossip!'

The village policeman was about to retire. He had been in the village for thirty years and was just about the most unpopular figure there. It was his proud boast that he had booked every resident in the village at some time or another, usually for some very minor infringement. The only man he had never been able to catch out was the local vicar, and he determined to rectify this omission before his retirement became due. The task seemed hopeless but as he watched the vicar cycling by one day, he hit upon a plan. He hid in some bushes at the bottom of a steep hill just outside the village and waited for the vicar to come cycling down. His plan was to dash out just at the last moment so that the vicar would run over his foot and he could have him for riding with faulty brakes.

He waited for over an hour but then at last the vicar came pedalling down the hill. As he drew near, the policeman dashed out from the bushes – but the vicar's reflexes were good and he pulled up about three inches from the constable's foot. 'Well,' said the policeman, 'I thought I had you there, vicar, I really did.'

'Ah, yes, but you see,' said the vicar, smiling, 'God was with me!'

'Got you at last!' said the bobbie. 'Two on a bike!'

Young Jimmy Smith was called into the headmaster's office because his teacher had reported him for using bad language. 'What exactly did you say?' asked the headmaster.

'Oh, I couldn't use them words in front of you, sir!' said Jimmy.

'Jimmy, I want to know exactly what swear words you used.'

'Well, sir,' said Jimmy, 'if you tell me a few of the ones you use yourself, I'll tell you when you come to the ones I used.'

A very devout vicar got married to an attractive young lady. On their wedding night, she went up to their room first, in order to prepare herself, and he followed half an hour later. Entering the bedroom, he found his bride, attired in a sexy nightgown, lying seductively on the bed. 'I had hoped, my dear,' he said, 'to find you on your knees at the side of the bed.'

'Well, all right,' said his bride, 'if you want me to – but doing it that way, I always get the hiccups.'

A young medical student halfway through his course developed a sore throat. He decided he knew enough

---

about medicine to write out his own prescription which he duly handed in at the chemist's. The chemist read it through carefully and then said doubtfully, 'Is it a very large dog, sir?'

The trial had been going on for three hours when the judge suddenly noticed that there were only eleven people in the jury box. 'Where is the twelfth man?' he asked the foreman of the jury.

'He had to go away on business,' said the foreman, 'but it's all right – he left his verdict with me.'

'I'm prescribing these pills for you,' said the doctor to the grossly overweight patient, who tipped the scales at about seventeen stone. 'I don't want you to swallow them. Just spill them on the floor twice a day and pick them up one at a time.'

A holidaymaker in America visited a Red Indian reservation and bought a peace pipe. He noticed some writing on the side of the pipe but the words were too small to make out. He turned to the Indian who had sold him the pipe and asked him what the words meant. The Indian examined it carefully, looked up, and said, 'It says, "Smoking can damage your health." '

It is reported that the old Duke of Gloucester once visited Cairo and was taken to see a display of belly-dancing. After the performance, he was taken round and introduced to the performer. There was a long silence while the Duke sought for some common ground on which to open the conversation. Finally he said, 'Do you know Tidworth?'

A group of hunters in the depths of an African forest decided to split up and meet back in the clearing three hours later. It was agreed that if any one of them got lost, he would shoot three times into the air to alert the others.

After about an hour, one member of the party found himself hopelessly lost so, as arranged, he shot three times into the air. Nothing happened, so he shot three times more. Again nobody came. 'I hope someone comes soon,' he muttered to himself, 'I've nearly run out of arrows.'

A married couple went away for a fortnight in the sun and arranged for their dog to be boarded in kennels. On their return, the husband went round and collected the dog and brought it home. 'I don't know what's got into Buster,' he said when he got in. 'He barked and struggled all the way home. I think he must be sickening for something.'

'It's not that,' said his wife. 'What he's been trying to tell you is that he's the wrong dog.'

A small boy returned home from his first day at school and proudly announced, 'We started maths today, Daddy.'

'Great,' said his father. 'What's one and one?'

'Er,' the little boy hesitated, 'we haven't got that far yet.'

It was a freezing cold day in the snow-covered steppes of Siberia. A young lad was walking along when he spotted a tiny bird being chased by a fox. The boy picked up the bird and, just at that moment, a horse came along and left a large deposit in the road. The boy scooped out a hole in the deposit and carefully placed the bird in it. It was warm and comfortable there and the bird soon recovered its spirits and poked its head out of the hole and began to sing with joy. But the hungry fox was still lurking nearby and it pounced on the little bird and gobbled it up.

The moral of this story is two-fold. First, it is not always your enemies who drop you in it. And, second, if you are up to your neck in it, keep your mouth shut!

There is a story about Dorothy Parker, the American wit, whose maid handed in her notice when she came in one day and found an alligator in the bath. She left the following note for Miss Parker: 'I cannot work in a house where there is an alligator in the bath. I would have mentioned this when I first took the job but I didn't think the matter would ever come up.'